Open Up 2.0

Grammar & Vocabulary 2

Clare Kennedy

CAMBRIDGE UNIVERSITY PRESS

Codice di sblocco 722-E17-0D3-9B9

IL LIBRO IN DIGITALE

Questo corso è distribuito sulla piattaforma MybSmart per computer e tablet.

❶ REGISTRATI SU IMPAROSULWEB

Vai sul sito *imparosulweb.eu* e registrati scegliendo il tuo profilo. Completa l'attivazione cliccando il link contenuto nell'e-mail di conferma. Al termine della procedura sarai indirizzato nella tua area personale.

❷ SBLOCCA IL VOLUME

Usa il **codice di sblocco** che trovi stampato su questo libro per sbloccarlo su Imparosulweb e per accedere anche alle espansioni online associate.

❸ SCARICA L'APPLICAZIONE MYBSMART

Clicca sul pulsante **Libro digitale** e segui le istruzioni per scaricare e installare l'applicazione.

❹ SCARICA IL LIBRO ATTIVATO

Entra nella libreria di MybSmart facendo login con il tuo account Imparosulweb e clicca sulla copertina del libro attivato per scaricarlo. Sfoglia le pagine e i pulsanti ti guideranno alla scoperta delle risorse multimediali collegate.

Sede operativa Via Vittorio Amedeo II, 18 - 10121 Torino
cambridge.org/cambridgeenglish - www.loescher.it

Ristampe	8	7	6	5	4	3	2
	2029	2028	2027	2026	2025	2024	2023

ISBN 9788858345818

Coordinamento editoriale: Mario Sacco
Realizzazione editoriale e tecnica: Fregi e Majuscole - Torino
Ricerca iconografica: Fregi e Majuscole - Torino
Progetto grafico: Fregi e Majuscole - Torino; Cambridge University Press
Copertina: Massimo Principi adv - Torino
Fotolito: Walter Bassani - Bascapè (PV)
Stampa: Sograte Litografia s.r.l. - Zona Industriale Regnano - 06012 Città di Castello (PG)

Contents

Vocabulary Review

TV and Cinema

1 ★☆☆ Completa i generi di film con la parte finale corretta (A–H).

_B_	anim*ation*	4 ___	act______
1 ___	historical ______	5 ___	musi______
2 ___	adven______	6 ___	rom______
3 ___	science ______	7 ___	com______

A ion **B** ation **C** edy **D** cal **E** antic **F** drama **G** ture **H** fiction

2 ★☆☆ Completa i nomi dei programmi TV.

RE *ALIT* Y *S* HOW

1 CH ___ ___ S ___ ___ W
2 ___ ___ ___ E C T ___ ___ E S E R ___ ___ ___
3 D ___ C ___ M ___ N T ___ ___ Y
4 Q ___ ___ Z ___ HO ___
5 SIT ___ ___ ___
6 ___ OA ___ ___ PER ___
7 ___ ___ OR _ S
8 T ___ E N ___ W ___

Food and Drink

3 ★☆☆ Completa la mappa con i nomi di cibo del riquadro.

~~cheese~~ oil grapes tomatoes orange juice lettuce ham tea chicken crisps pears rice

FOOD

- Fruit: ______ / ______
- Vegetables: ______ / ______
- Meat: ______ / ______
- Snacks: *cheese* / ______
- Basics: ______ / ______
- Drink: ______ / ______

4 ★★☆ Completa con i nomi dei contenitori.

a bag of apples

1 ____________ of crisps

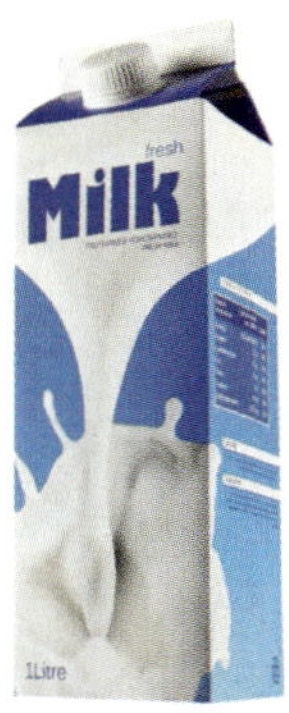

2 ____________ milk

3 ____________ orange juice

4 ____________ cola

5 ____________ water

6 ____________ coffee

7 ____________ tea

8 ____________ honey

9 ____________ eggs

Vocabulary Round-up

5 ★★★ **Completa il testo con le parole del riquadro.**

clips documentary films make show programmes questions watching ~~club~~

This year I go to Media club at school. It's really cool! Every week, we learn about different kinds of media like radio, television, [1]__________ and the internet. At the moment, we're [2]__________ different kinds of TV [3]__________ . The teachers usually show us short [4]__________ from the programmes. They talk about them and ask us [5]__________ . I'm learning a lot about making TV programmes! Now, we're ready to [6]__________ our own TV [7]__________ ! It's a [8]__________ about our school.

6 ★★★ **Leggi i commenti e abbinali ai generi di film e ai programmi TV. Ci sono due opzioni in più.**

1 A Max I never go to the cinema but I love watching films at home. I like watching films about life in the future and especially on different planets!

2 ___ Daisy I don't spend a lot of time watching films and TV but there's one show I love. It's about a group of real people learning how to dance. All my friends are fans too.

3 ___ Oliver I like TV and I watch it with my brother. We love watching matches and competitions with our favourite teams and players. We don't watch any other channels!

4 ___ Lola I'm a film fan and I love going to the cinema with my friends. We see all the new films when they come out. We watch all types of films except action movies and our favourite films are love stories.

A science fiction films
B documentaries
C reality shows
D sports programmes
E animation films
F romantic films

7 ★★★ **Cerchia l'opzione corretta.**

A Have you got the list of *ingredients* / *containers* for the cake?
B Yes, here it is. First of all, butter.
A Butter. Where's that?
B With the [1] ***milk products*** / ***vegetables***, I think.
A Ah yes. Next, we need a [2] ***box*** / ***bag*** of eggs.
B Here they are. What else do we need for the cake?
A [3] ***Sugar*** / ***Sausages***.
B A one-kilo [4] ***packet*** / ***can***?
A Yes, that's fine. Now a jar of [5] ***jam*** / ***ham***. I think that's all.
B No, it isn't! What about the strawberries?
B Oh, yes. Strawberries. There're with the [6] ***fruit*** / ***meat***.
A And drinks? Let's get some [7] ***fruit juice*** / ***courgettes***.
B OK. How many [8] ***bottles*** / ***cups***?
A Two. That's fine.

8 ★★★ **Leggi le informazioni e scegli la risposta corretta (A, B o C).**

When you go to the shops, please, can you buy some tomatoes, lettuce, and cheese? Thanks.
08:32

This is … .
A an action film
B a romantic film
C science fiction

1 Milly wants to make … .
A a cake
B beefburgers
C a salad

Beefburgers
Cheese sandwiches
Chips
Pancakes with jam

2 You see this in a … .
A sweet shop
B cinema
C restaurant

3 These are all … .
A breakfast food
B snacks
C sweet

Grammar Review

1 ★ Scrivi se le regole si riferiscono al *present simple* (PS) o al *present continuous* (PC).

1 ____ azioni in corso nel momento in cui si parla
2 ____ con avverbi di frequenza
3 ____ con espressioni come *at the moment*
4 ____ azioni abituali

2 ★★ Scrivi le frasi usando il *present simple* o il *present continuous*.

I / always / drink / milk / breakfast
I always drink milk for breakfast.

1 My friends / play / in the park / now
2 You / often / watch / films?
3 Amy / not / dance right now
4 We / never / go/ to the cinema

3 ★ Cerchia l'opzione corretta per completare la regola sui verbi *like* / *enjoy* / *love* / *hate*.

like / *enjoy* / *love* / *hate* e altri verbi che esprimono gusti personali di solito sono seguiti da:

- [1]*sostantivi* / *aggettivi*
- [2]*forma -ing* / *infinito*

4 ★★ Completa le frasi con i verbi del riquadro.

enjoy ~~play~~ shop tidy watch

Jack loves *playing* tennis.

1 I hate ________________ my room.
2 The students ________________ music lessons. They're fun!
3 We love ________________ on Saturdays!
4 Do you like ________________ TV?

5 ★ Completa le regole sugli avverbi di modo con le parole del riquadro.

badly -ily well -ly

- Aggettivi regolari: → + [1]______
- Aggettivi che terminano in *-y*: → + [2]______
- Aggettivi irregolari, ad esempio:
  good: → [3]______ bad: → [4]______

6 ★ Cambia gli aggettivi in avverbi di modo.

The cars are moving *slowly* (slow).

1 Nina can run very ________________ (fast).
2 Can you speak ________________ (quiet) please?
3 We win all our matches ________________ (easy).
4 Sam plays the guitar very ________________ (good).

7 ★ I sostantivi sono numerabili (C = *countable*) o non numerabili (U = *uncountable*)?

book *C*

1 water	____	5 milk	____
2 cheese	____	6 egg	____
3 tomato	____	7 cup	____
4 pen	____	8 coffee	____

8 ★ Cerchia l'opzione corretta per completare le regole su *some* / *any*. In un caso ci sono due opzioni corrette.

- Si usano *some* / *any* per quantità [1]***precisate* / *imprecisate***.
- Si usa *some* nelle frasi [2]***affermative*/ *negative*** e nelle frasi [3]***affermative* / *negative* / *interrogative***.

9 ★ Completa le frasi con *some* o *any*.

I've got *some* new shoes!

1 Have you got ______ sandwiches?
2 There's ______ apple juice in the fridge.
3 We haven't got ______ biscuits.
4 There are ______ girls in the science lab.

10 ★ Completa le regole su *a lot of* / *much* / *many* con le parole del riquadro.

much a lot of many grandi

- *much*, *many* e *a lot of* si usano per [1]______ quantità.
- Si usa [2]______ con i sostantivi numerabili e [3]______ con i sostantivi non numerabili.
- Si usa [4]______ con i sostantivi sia numerabili sia non numerabili.

11 ★ Cerchia l'opzione corretta: *much* o *many*.

How *much* / *many* butter do you need?

1 Are there *much* / *a lot of* students in your class?
2 There aren't *much* / *many* eggs in the box.
3 How *much* / *many* children are there?
4 How *much* / *many* rice do you usually eat?

12 ★ Cerchia l'opzione corretta per completare le regole su *a few* / *a little*.

- *a few* / *a little* si usano per [1]***piccole* / *grandi*** quantità.
- Si usa *a little* con i sostantivi [2]***numerabili* / *non numerabili*** e *a few* con i sostantivi [3]***numerabili* / *non numerabili***.

13 ★ Completa le frasi con *a few* o *a little*.

There are *a few* apples in the box.

1 I've got ______ water in my bottle.
2 I only like ______ vegetables.
3 Have you got ______ chocolate for me?
4 Can we have ______ chips, please?

Grammar Round-up

14 ★★★ **Completa il dialogo con la forma corretta dei verbi tra parentesi.**

A What *are you doing* ? (you / do)
B I [1] ________ (wait) for my sister. She's late so I [2] ________ (watch) a video.
A What's it about?
B Food in different countries.
A Do you [3] ________ (like / watch) videos about food?
B Yes, I do. I [4] ________ (follow) this one.
A [5] ________ (it / show) you what people eat?
B That's right. In every episode, they [6] ________ (visit) a family at home and they [7] ________ (talk) about the food they eat.
A Let's see. What [8] ________ (they / make) now?
B They [9] ________ (cook) their dinner. See, they [10] ________ (explain) how to make it.

15 ★★★ **Scegli la risposta corretta (A, B o C).**

A How ___ TV do you watch?
B Actually, I watch very [1] ___ TV.
A Really? I enjoy [2] ___ TV with my family or [3] ___ friends.
B I prefer TV series online.
A How [4] ___ episodes do you watch at a time?
B I often [5] ___ three or four in an evening.
A Really? I [6] ___ do that! I don't [7] ___ staying in my room alone.
B Well, I sometimes watch a film with a [8] ___ friends.

	A old	(**B**) much	**C** many
1	**A** small	**B** little	**C** few
2	**A** watches	**B** watching	**C** watch
3	**A** much	**B** some	**C** many
4	**A** many	**B** little	**C** much
5	**A** seeing	**B** sees	**C** see
6	**A** always	**B** never	**C** ever
7	**A** liking	**B** likes	**C** like
8	**A** few	**B** little	**C** some

16 ★★★ **Completa il testo con le parole del riquadro.**

always cook ~~cooking~~ few enjoy do doesn't some go 'm looking trying

I love *cooking* . It's my hobby and I often [1] ________ for my family. I like [2] ________ new recipes. Where [3] ________ I find my recipes? I've got a [4] ________ recipe books and I follow [5] ________ food vloggers. I [6] ________ food shopping too so I always [7] ________ to the shops and buy the ingredients. Mum and Dad [8] ________ enjoy my food but sometimes my little sister [9] ________ like it. At the moment, I [10] ________ for a recipe for her birthday cake.

17 ★★★ **Completa il testo con una parola per spazio.**

This is the first week of my family's healthy eating plan! We don't have *any* fast food now and I'm trying to eat a [1] ________ of fresh vegetables. We don't eat [2] ________ meat but we have [3] ________ fish. We also have a [4] ________ cheese and a [5] ________ eggs – but not a lot. How [6] ________ fruit do we have? Well, we don't have [7] ________ cakes so there's always [8] ________ lot of fresh fruit on the table.

18 ★★★ **Scrivi le domande e poi rispondi.**

How often / you / go / cinema?
How often do you go to the cinema?

1 How / TV / you / watch?
2 You / like / watch / reality shows?
3 You / like / cook?
4 How / fruit / your family / eat?
5 How / you / eat out?

After-school clubs

1 BEFORE YOU READ Rispondi alle domande.

1 What extra activities can you do at your school?
2 What clubs and activities do you do after school?

2 Leggi le informazioni su due attività extrascolastiche e completa la tabella.

FILM CLUB

When:
Thursday 4.00 – 5.00 pm. First Friday of the month: Movie Night

Where:
The main hall

Are you interested in films? Do you want to know about film-making? Then Film Club is for you!

We're interested in all kinds of films, from cartoons and animation to musicals and historical drama.

We watch short clips and then we talk about them together. There are lessons about the history of film-making too.

You can also help to choose the film for Movie Night! This is open to all students, so you can bring your friends!

COOKING CLUB

When: Tuesday 4.00 – 5.30 pm. Christmas, Easter, summer: Club Café

Where: Food technology Room 2

At cookery club, we don't just cook, we learn all about food! We teach you how to choose what to eat and how to cook. There are also lessons about different food with information about where it comes from and the good things it contains. Every two weeks, you cook a simple dish to take home. We give you the list of the ingredients you need and we cook it together in our kitchen.

Don't forget the Cooking Club Café – with all the food and drinks prepared by you!

	Film club	Cooking club
Day	Thursday	*Tuesday*
Time	1 ______	4.30 – 5.30
Place	Hall	2 ______
Activities	History of film making and 3 ______	Lessons about food and 4 ______
Extra activity	Once a month 5 ______	Three times a year 6 ______

3 Leggi di nuovo i testi dell'es. 2 e indica (✓) se le affermazioni (1–6) sono vere (T = *true*), false (F = *false*) o se la risposta non è deducibile dal testo (NG = *not given*). La prima risposta (0) è un esempio.

	T	F	NG
0 Film Club is one day a week.	✓		
1 You only watch films at Film Club.			
2 You sometimes learn about films from the past.			
3 The club organises trips to the cinema.			
4 Cooking club and Film Club are one hour long.			
5 You cook food at the club every week.			
6 You buy the ingredients at school.			

Hobbies

4 BEFORE YOUR READ Rispondi alle domande.

1 What are your hobbies?
2 Do you want to try a new hobby? What?

5 Leggi i testi e indica (✓) se le frasi sono vere (T = *true*) o false (F = *false*). Poi correggi quelle false.

My hobbies

Lucas

I've got a new hobby – it's gardening! I've got my own vegetable garden at my grandparent's house. They help me and teach me what to do. I usually go to see my garden after school. It's hard work and sometimes the plants don't grow very well. But I love working in the garden and some of the vegetables are nearly ready to eat now.

I go to a drama club because I'm interested in theatre and films. I'm not sure I want to be an actor but I'd really like to work in films. I'm in the beginners' group so we aren't doing a show. We're learning how to act and we're doing a lot of different exercises. I enjoy going to drama club, it's cool.

Stanley

Noah

I spend my free time watching films or reading about them – how they make films, the actors, the special effects and all the other things. I like having a souvenir of every film I see, so I collect cinema tickets. The problem is I can't collect digital tickets! So, now I sometimes buy old tickets for my collection. They're interesting too!

	T	F
1 Lucas's mum helps him with his hobby.	☐	☐
2 Stanley wants to be an actor in a theatre.	☐	☐
3 Noah has got two hobbies.	☐	☐

6 Leggi di nuovo i testi. Per ogni domanda cerchia la risposta corretta (A, B o C).

	Lucas	Stanley	Noah
1 Who does his hobby outdoors?	A	B	C
2 Who keeps old things for this hobby?	A	B	C
3 Who is thinking about his future?	A	B	C
4 Who is changing something about his hobby?	A	B	C
5 Who does his hobby every day?	A	B	C
6 Who produces food?	A	B	C
7 Who does his hobby with a group of people?	A	B	C

Listening and Writing

Listening

1 BEFORE YOU LISTEN Rispondi alle domande.

1 Do you enjoy parties? Why?
2 How do you celebrate your birthday?

2 02 **Ascolta due amici che parlano di una festa di compleanno e indica (✓) ciò di cui parlano.**

☐ party ☐ the time ☐ clothes ☐ food ☐ presents ☐ films

3 03 **Ascolta di nuovo. Durante l'ascolto, indica (✓) la risposta corretta (A, B, C o D) per le domande 1–4. Solo una risposta è corretta. La prima risposta (0) è un esempio. Ascolterai la registrazione due volte.**

0 What type of film do they choose?

1 What time does the film start?

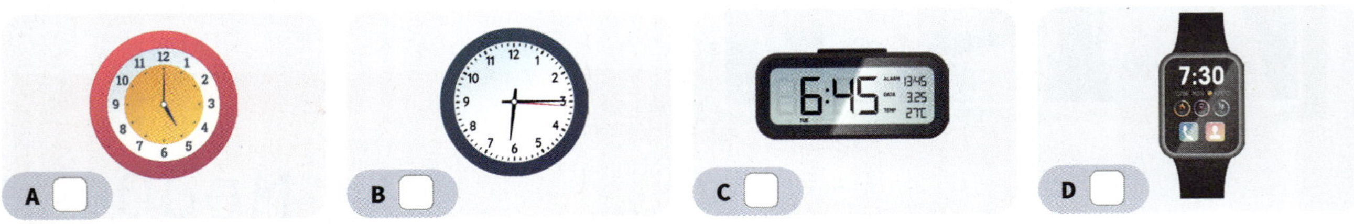

2 What's the name of the café?

3 What food do they choose?

4 What do they eat at Jade's house?

4 BEFORE YOU LISTEN Rispondi alle domande.

1 Do you enjoy going to museums? Why?

2 Where is a good place to visit on a school trip?

5 04 Ascolta un insegnante che parla alla classe di una gita. Cerchia l'opzione corretta.

1 The trip starts in the *morning* / *afternoon*.

2 They have a *picnic* / *snack in a café*.

3 They need money to buy *souvenirs* / *tickets*.

6 04 Ascolta di nuovo. Completa le informazioni. Scrivi una parola, un numero, una data o un'ora.

Trip to the Film Museum

The trip starts at [1]__________ .

There's an exhibition about film [2]__________ .

You can watch [3]__________ parts of films.

Please bring a small [4]__________ .

You need some money for [5]__________ and souvenirs from the shop.

Writing

7 Leggi la traccia con attenzione e scrivi il messaggio.

You want to invite some friends to your house on your birthday. Write a message to your friends to tell them about your plans.

In your message:

- invite your friends
- tell them which film you want to watch
- tell them about the food

B Units 3–4

Vocabulary Review

Appearance and Parts of the body

1 ★★★ Scrivi le parole del riquadro nella categoria corretta.

~~ear~~ arm freckles mouth chest
beard knee nose elbow eye hand
chin foot forehead ankle eyebrow

HEAD	BODY
ear	______
______	______
______	______
______	______
______	______
______	______
______	______
______	______

2 ★★★ Completa le parole relative all'aspetto fisico.

0 H *A I R*	6 G _ _ _ _ _ _
1 E _ _	7 N _ _ _
2 E _ _	8 M _ _ _ _
3 M _ _ _ _ _ _ _	9 C _ _ _
4 B _ _ _ _	10 N _ _ _
5 S _ _ _ _ _ _ _	11 C _ _ _ _

3 ★★★ Cerchia l'intruso.

	fringe	spiky	(elbow)	long
1	ankle	mouth	knee	leg
2	chin	wavy	chest	knee
3	beard	neck	moustache	hair
4	forehead	blond	dark	grey
5	hands	feet	legs	head

Feelings and Personality

4 ★★★ Le seguenti emozioni sono positive (P) o negative (N)?

afraid *N*		5 relaxed ___
1 angry ___		6 sad ___
2 bored ___		7 surprised ___
3 excited ___		8 tired ___
4 happy ___		9 worried ___

5 ★★★ Completa gli aggettivi relativi alla personalità.

F U *N N* Y

1 SER _ _ _ _	7 BO _ _ _
2 FRIE _ _ _ _	8 AN _ _ _
3 KI _ _	9 SUR _ _ _ _ _ _
4 BR _ _ _	10 WOR _ _ _ _
5 QU _ _ _	11 TI _ _ _
6 S _ _	12 AF _ _ _ _

6 ★★★ Osserva le immagini e scrivi un aggettivo che esprima le emozioni che vedi. Sono possibili più risposte.

tired

1 ______________

2 ______________

3 ______________

Vocabulary Round-up

7 ★★ **Leggi le descrizioni e scegli l'aggettivo corretto (A, B o C).**

1
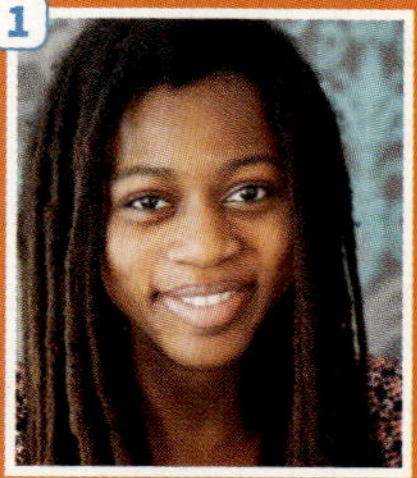

Abbie's very nice. She's never worried or angry. She's usually quiet and relaxed. She's a very ___ person.

A excited **B** calm **C** nervous

2
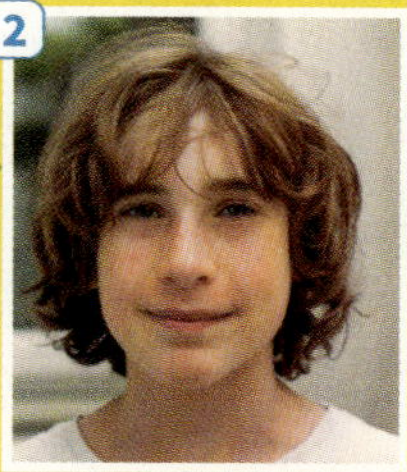

Jordan likes to be quiet and alone. He's a bit nervous of other people. I think he's ___ .

A shy **B** kind **C** clever

3

Henry likes people and he's very popular. He's kind and enjoys helping other people too. He's a ___ kid.

A shy **B** friendly **C** brave

4

Chloe isn't afraid of dangerous or difficult things! She loves adventures and trying new activities. She's a really ___ girl.

A funny **B** calm **C** brave

5
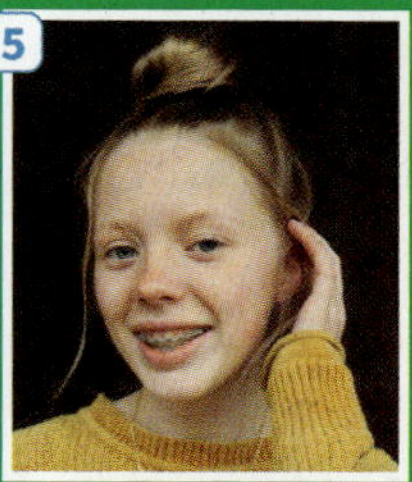

Milly talks a lot and her stories make us laugh. Her favourite films are comedies. We all have fun when Milly's around. We think Milly's ___ .

A nervous **B** funny **C** clever

8 ★★ **Completa le frasi con una parola per spazio.**

Your *nose* is in the middle of your face, above your mouth.

1 Your ________ are at the end of your arms.
2 Your ________ is between your leg and your foot.
3 Your ________ is between your head and your chest.
4 Your ________ are on the side of your head.
5 Your ________ is in the middle of your leg.
6 ________ are small brown spots on your face.
7 ________ help you to see better.
8 A ________ is hair on a man's chin.

9 ★★★ **Come ti senti in queste situazioni? Cerchia l'opzione corretta.**

You watch a horror film on a dark night. ***afraid* / *angry***

1 Your friends organise a secret party for your birthday. ***bored* / *surprised***
2 You've got a test tomorrow but you don't know anything. ***worried* / *happy***
3 You're going on your summer holiday tomorrow. ***excited* / *sad***
4 You're on the beach on a hot, sunny day. ***worried* / *relaxed***
5 Your sister used your camera and broke it. ***angry* / *tired***
6 It's the end of a very busy day. ***tired* / *surprised***

10 ★★★ **Osserva l'immagine e descrivi le persone raffigurate.**

1 What does he / she look like?
2 What do you think his / her personality is like?
3 How is he / she feeling now?

Grammar Review

1 ★ Completa la tabella con il *past simple* di *be*.

	Forma affermativa	Forma negativa
I / He / She / It	1 ______	3 ______
We / You / They	2 ______	4 ______
	Forma interrogativa	
I / He / She / It	5 ______ he?	
We / You / They	6 ______ they?	

2 ★ Completa le frasi con la forma affermativa (+) o negativa (–) del *past simple* di *be*.

We *weren't* at school yesterday. It was Sunday.

1 I ______ born on 24 November. (+)
2 You ______ very late for the lesson. (+)
3 My bag ______ in my room. (–)
4 My friends ______ at the park yesterday. (–)

3 ★★ Scrivi le domande al *past simple* e rispondi usando i suggerimenti.

You / late? Yes
Were you late? Yes, I was.

1 your friends / at home? No
2 the bus / late? Yes
3 Alex / happy? No
4 the children / park? Yes

4 ★ Scrivi la struttura delle domande introdotte dalle parole interrogative.

soggetto *was / were* *Wh-*

1 ______	2 ______	3 ______

5 ★★ Scrivi le domande usando i suggerimenti e *was* o *were*.

How many / people / there?
How many people were there?

1 What / the time?
2 Where / the bags?
3 How old / you?
4 Why / the lesson late?

6 ★ Completa la regola del *past simple* di *have* con le parole del riquadro.

have / has had

Il *past simple* di [1] ______ è [2] ______ .

7 ★ Completa le frasi con *have*, *has* o *had*.

I *had* my birthday party last Saturday.

1 Kate ______ short hair last year.
2 We ______ English lessons twice a week this year.
3 My sister ______ blue eyes and blond hair.
4 They ______ sushi for dinner yesterday.

8 ★ Completa la regola sul *past simple* dei verbi regolari.

Il *past simple* dei verbi regolari si forma aggiungendo [1] ______ alla forma base del verbo. Per esempio, *walk* → [2] ______

9 ★★ Completa con il *past simple* dei verbi tra parentesi.

The match *started* at 3 pm. (start)

1 We ______ the dinner yesterday. (cook)
2 I ______ my dad in the garden. (help)
3 Matt ______ tennis all morning. (play)
4 You ______ a lot of questions! (ask)

10 ★ Cerchia l'opzione corretta per completare le regole ortografiche sul *past simple* dei verbi regolari.

Se il verbo finisce con:

- -*e* (per esempio, *change*)
  → si aggiunge [1] (*-d*) / *-ed*.
- consonante + -*y* (per esempio, *study*):
  → si usa la desinenza [2] *-ied* / *-ed*.
- vocale + consonante (per esempio, *stop*):
  → si raddoppia la [3] *vocale* / *consonante*.

11 ★ Scrivi il *past simple* dei seguenti verbi regolari.

like *liked*

1 arrive ______ 4 plan ______
2 carry ______ 5 try ______
3 chat ______ 6 live ______

12 ★★ Scrivi il *past simple* dei seguenti verbi irregolari.

drink *drank*

1 buy ______ 4 write ______
2 eat ______ 5 make ______
3 go ______ 6 speak ______

Grammar Round-up

13 ★★ **Riscrivi le frasi al *present simple* o al *past simple*.**

My family lives in a house now.

My family *lived* in a flat three years ago.

1 I went out with my friends last Saturday.
I ______________ every Saturday.

2 Dad cooked dinner yesterday.
Dad always ______________.

3 My birthday was a week ago.
My birthday ______________ in April.

4 We always meet our friends in the park.
We ______________ last Friday.

5 Lucy sometimes plays video games in the evening.
Lucy ______________ yesterday.

6 You were my best friend at primary school.
You ______________ now!

14 ★★ **Scegli la risposta corretta (A, B o C).**

Lucy	Where were you ___ afternoon?
Jamil	I [1]___ at the sports centre. Why?
Lucy	I [2]___ to speak to you.
Jamil	[3]___ it important?
Lucy	No, not really.
Jamil	I [4]___ about Ed's accident.
Lucy	Poor Ed. He [5]___ his foot.
Jamil	[6]___ he at home now?
Lucy	Yes, but he can't [7]___ .
Jamil	I [8]___ about visiting him yesterday.
Lucy	Let's go after school today!

	A	B	C
	A last	B today	(C) yesterday
1	A was	B were	C am
2	A want	B wants	C wanted
3	A Is	B Was	C Are
4	A heard	B hearing	C hears
5	A breaking	B breaks	C broke
6	A Were	B Is	C Was
7	A walk	B walked	C walks
8	A think	B taught	C thought

15 ★★ **Completa il dialogo con la forma corretta dei verbi nel riquadro.**

drive ~~go~~ arrive not be (x2) fall phone tell hurt

Last week I *went* for a bike ride with my friend Josh.

He [1]______________ off his bike on the way home and [2]______________ his leg!

He couldn't stand up. I [3]______________ sure what to do. There [4]______________ any people around to help, so I [5]______________ Josh's mum. She [6]______________ me to wait with Josh. She [7]______________ quickly and [8]______________ him to the hospital.

16 ★★★ **Completa il testo con una parola per spazio.**

I met Cleo on *the* first day of primary school. We immediately became friends and she's [1]______________ best friend now! What does she look [2]______________ ? Well, she's tall and she's [3]______________ blond hair and blue eyes. She [4]______________ long hair before but she cut it short last year. [5]______________ looks cool with her short, spiky hair! A few years [6]______________, she was shy but now she isn't! I think she's clever [7]______________ she's serious about her school work. She's interested in the same things as [8]______________ so we always have fun together.

17 ★★★ **Scrivi le domande e poi rispondi.**

Where / you born?
Where were you born?

1 Where / your primary school?
____

2 What / name / your primary school?
____

3 Who / first teachers?
____

4 What / favourite subject at primary school?
____

5 Who / your friends at primary school?
____

6 What / favourite games?
____

Reading

A school trip

1 BEFORE YOU READ Rispondi alle domande.

1 Where was your last holiday?

2 Was it a good holiday? Why?

2 Leggi il resoconto della gita di Ruby e indica (✓) il riassunto corretto (A o B).

Adventure week-end

Last weekend was very special! My class went on a trip to an adventure centre and it was fantastic!

I couldn't sleep the night before because I was so excited – and a bit worried about the new activities. We left early on Friday morning and arrived back at school late on Sunday. The adventure centre was in a big house in the country. The bedrooms had six beds – so we had fun together in our room! We had our breakfast and dinner there but we spent all day outside. We tried a lot of different activities: climbing was my favourite. We started on a climbing wall in the gym and then we went out on the rocks! We also tried canoeing, mountain-biking and horse-riding! I was a bit afraid of the horse. This sport isn't for me – I wasn't relaxed at all! The teachers were all really friendly and helped us a lot.

In the evenings we were very hungry and tired – but happy. There was a tasty dinner and then quizzes, games and films. We were certainly never bored!

We went to bed quite early because we were very tired. My legs and arms hurt a bit after climbing, but that was all. One of my friends cut his knee badly on the first day but it wasn't serious.

We enjoyed the weekend so much that we want to go back there soon!

A ☐ Ruby spent a week at an adventure centre with her family. Her favourite activity was horse-riding. She was a bit bored in the evenings so she wants to go on a different holiday next year.

B ☐ Ruby spent a few days at an adventure centre with her school friends. She liked climbing but not horse-riding. At the end of every day, she felt tired but happy. She wants to go on another holiday like this.

3 Leggi di nuovo il resoconto della gita di Ruby e rispondi alle domande (1–6). Usa quattro parole al massimo. La prima risposta (0) è un esempio. I

0 When was the school trip? *last weekend.*

1 How was Ruby before the trip? __________

2 How long was the trip? __________

3 Where was the adventure centre? __________

4 What were the teachers like? __________

5 Which activity was difficult for Ruby? __________

6 What do Ruby and her classmates hope to do? __________

An exciting experience

4 BEFORE YOU READ Rispondi alle domande.

1 When was the last time you went on a trip with your family?
2 What was your best day out ever?

5 Leggi il testo e completa gli appunti.

A GREAT DAY OUT

What was my best day out ever? It was on my birthday last year when I was thirteen. My uncle took me to watch a Formula One race! I was so excited!

The day started early. My uncle and cousin, Daniel, came to get me and we drove to the race track. The journey took about two hours but it went quickly because we talked non-stop about cars and the race. The race track was enormous and it was full of people, trucks and cars. We walked around and looked at all the different things. After a snack in a café, we went to find our seats. They were in a great position, high up and near the start. I wasn't bored for a minute because I could see the preparations for the race. Then, the cars and the teams came out. We saw all the famous drivers and I took lots of photos.

Finally, the race started! The cars made a lot of noise and I put my hands over my ears! I was surprised because when you watch a race on TV, you don't hear the noise. And another thing, the cars go so fast – they fly past in a few seconds. I watched the race again on TV when I got home because I wanted to see all of it. I only saw the part in front of us. It was a great race and my favourite driver won it.

It was the perfect day for me!

Luke's trip

When?
1 Last year on ____________________

Where?
2 ____________________

Who with?
3 ____________________

Luke's opinion
4 ____________________

6 Rileggi il testo e indica (✓) la risposta corretta (A, B o C).

1 Luke's special day out was a trip to … .
- A ☐ birthday party
- B ☑ a sports event
- C ☐ his cousin's house

2 Where was the race?
- A ☐ Near Luke's home.
- B ☐ A few kilometres away.
- C ☐ A long distance away.

3 What was the place like?
- A ☐ Big and busy.
- B ☐ Full of traffic.
- C ☐ Small with places to eat.

4 Before the race started, they … .
- A ☐ watched people get everything ready
- B ☐ looked at photos and chatted
- C ☐ spoke to some famous drivers

5 Luke was surprised that … .
- A ☐ his favourite team won
- B ☐ the cars weren't very fast
- C ☐ some things were different from on TV

Listening and Writing

Listening

1 BEFORE YOU LISTEN Rispondi alle domande.

1 Where do you go on holiday?
2 Do you ever make new friends on holiday?

2 05 Ascolta Liam che descrive una foto scattata durante le vacanze e indica (✓) i nomi che senti.

- [ ] Johnny
- [ ] Billy
- [ ] Oliver
- [ ] Alice
- [ ] Jenny
- [ ] Martha
- [ ] Lily

3 06 Ascolta di nuovo. Scrivi i nomi delle persone negli spazi 1–4. La prima risposta (0) è un esempio. Ascolterai la registrazione due volte.

0 *Billy*

1 ______

2 ______

3 ______

4 ______

4 BEFORE YOU LISTEN Rispondi alle domande.

1 What's your personality like?

2 Have your friends got different personalities from you?

5 07 Ascolta Marcus che descrive a una nuova studentessa, Lara, alcuni compagni di classe. Numera gli aggettivi nell'ordine in cui li senti nominare.

☐ different ☐ difficult ☐ intelligent ☐ interesting ☐ normal ☐ popular

6 08 Ascolta di nuovo. Durante l'ascolto, abbina le persone (1–5) alle personalità (A–H). Ci sono due personalità in più. Ascolterai la registrazione due volte.

People		**Personality**
1 ___	Nick	**A** brave
2 ___	Andy	**B** funny
3 ___	Poppy	**C** kind
4 ___	Zara	**D** friendly
5 ___	Harry	**E** quiet
		F serious
		G clever

Writing

7 Leggi la traccia con attenzione e scrivi il messaggio.

You want to tell your English-speaking cousin about your new friend. Write a message to your cousin to tell him / her about your new friend.

In your message:

- give some information: name, age, where from
- describe what your friend looks like
- tell your cousin about his / her personality and interests

Vocabulary Review

Holidays, Activities and People

1 ★ **Scrivi le parole del riquadro nella colonna corretta.**

island lake map mountain passport sea sightseeing backpacker beach ~~camera~~ cycling flip flops hiker surfing skiing suitcase goggles towel sunglasses ~~sun cream~~ swimming

HOLIDAYS

Holidays things
camera
______
______
______

Beach things
sun cream
______
______
______
______

People
______
______

Places
______
______
______
______
______

Activities
______
______
______
______
______

2 ★ **Completa le parole relative alle vacanze.**

glasses suit pack seeing sun

back*pack*
1 sun______
2 sight______
3 swim______
4 ______hat

Places in towns and cities, Shops and Giving directions

3 ★ **Scrivi il nome dei negozi che vendono i seguenti articoli.**

bookshop

1 ______

2 ______

3 ______

4 ______

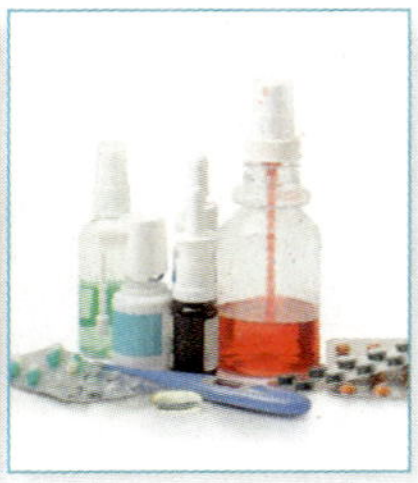
5 ______

4 ★ **Abbina e componi i nomi di luoghi di città.**

D	car	**A** shop
1 ___	bus	**B** station
2 ___	book	**C** stop
3 ___	police	**D** park
4 ___	cross	**E** about
5 ___	traffic	**F** roads
6 ___	zebra	**G** crossing
7 ___	round	**H** lights

5 ★★ **Aggiungi tre parole per ciascuna categoria.**

Directions: traffic lights *bridge* *crossroads* *zebra crossing*

1 Places in towns and cities:
library ______
______ ______

2 Shops:
chemist's ______
______ ______

Vocabulary Round-up

6 ★★☆ **Dove sono? Leggi la descrizione e completa.**

Christina There are people studying here. You can choose a book and take it home. After two weeks, you bring it back and choose a different book. I'm in a *library* .

Anna I'm in town. I want to post a birthday card to my friend. There are other people in here. They want to post parcels and letters. I'm in a 1 ______________ .

Jasmine I'm on a bike ride and I need to cross a river. I go up the road and then I go down on the other side. I'm on a 2 ______________ .

William I'm on a small place in the sea. There is water all around me. I came here by boat. I'm on an 3 ______________ .

Tim This place is very big and there are hundreds of people here today. You can only enter with a ticket. We're watching a sports match. I'm in a 4 ______________ .

7 ★★☆ **Scegli la risposta corretta (A, B o C).**

Last week my class visited the Jurassic Coast in Dorset. Our ___ was in a small 1___ . It was near a church and a 2___ over the river. On the first day, we went to visit the 3___ . It had a lot of very old things including fossils and dinosaur bones! The next day, we went to the sea. We walked along the 4___ to look at the famous rocks. Our teacher had a 5___ so we could find the interesting places. I took some photos with my new 6___ . We took our 7___ and sunhats because it was very hot! In the afternoon, we went 8___ in the sea.

	A	B	C
	A campervan	(B) hotel	C crossroads
1	A lake	B town	C tunnel
2	A zebra crossing	B bridge	C towel
3	A museum	B church	C theatre
4	A island	B passport	C beach
5	A hiker	B map	C corner
6	A flip flop	B swimsuit	C camera
7	A backpacks	B backpackers	C swimsuits
8	A skiing	B cycling	C swimming

8 ★★☆ **Cerchia l'opzione corretta.**

A Do you know the way to the beach?

B Yes, sure. It isn't far from here. So walk (*along*) / *under* this road to the supermarket on the 1*tunnel* / *corner*. Then turn right at the 2*traffic lights* / *pavement*. When you get to the 3*corner* / *zebra crossing*, cross the road. Go 4*under* / *round* the bridge, then you'll see the sea! Walk along the 5*pavement* / *crossroads* and there's the entrance to the beach.

A Thanks very much!

9 ★★★ **Leggi i messaggi e scegli la risposta corretta.**

1

Can I meet you at the theatre and not the library? Then we can walk to the museum together. 16:12

Where are they going?

A To the theatre.
B To the library.
C To the museum.

2

THIS CAR PARK IS CLOSED TODAY.
Please use the car parks
at the leisure centre,
bus station and the art gallery.

What does this sign mean?

A You can leave your car here.
B No car parks are open today.
C Go to a different car park.

3

From: Harper

I'm in the town centre. I need to buy some flowers for Mum's birthday. Where can I go?

Harper's looking for ... .

A a florist's
B a greengrocer's
C a chemist's

4

Special Offer Holidays!

- Sun cream
- Sun glasses
- Sun hats
- Beach towels

All half price!

Where is this shop?

A In the mountains.
B At the sea.
C In the city centre.

Grammar Review

1 ★ Completa la regola della forma negativa del *past simple*.

- Soggetto + did not + forma ¹ ______ del verbo.
- Forma negativa contratta: ² ______________ + forma ³ ______________ del verbo.

2 ★ Scrivi le frasi usando la forma negativa del *past simple*.

I / go / sightseeing / yesterday
I didn't go sightseeing yesterday.

1 We / watch / the surfers
2 My friends / play / on the beach
3 Mark / enjoy / the holiday
4 You / take / a lot of photos

3 ★ Completa le regole della forma interrogativa e delle risposte brevi al *past simple*.

soggetto ~~Did~~ base

Did + ¹ __________ + forma ² __________ del verbo?

did didn't soggetto (x2)

Yes, ³ ______________ + ⁴ ______________ .

No, ⁵ ______________ + ⁶ ______________ .

4 ★★ Scrivi domande al *past simple* usando i suggerimenti.

you / go / on holiday / ?
Did you go on holiday? No, we didn't .

1 your brothers / swim / ?
______________________ ? Yes, ______________ .
2 Tom / visit / the castle / ?
______________________ ? Yes, ______________ .
3 she / buy / any souvenirs / ?
______________________ ? No, ______________ .
4 Nina / go / skiing / ?
______________________ ? No, ______________ .

5 ★ Completa la tabella del verbo *could*.

Forma affermativa
Soggetto + could + forma base del verbo.
Forma negativa
Soggetto + ¹ ______________ + forma base del verbo.
Forma interrogativa
² ______________ + soggetto + forma base del verbo?
Risposte brevi
Yes, you ³ ______________ . No, they ⁴ ______________ .

6 ★ Completa le frasi con *could* o *couldn't*.

Could you swim when you were ten?

1 I ______________ ski when I was six but I can now!
2 It was fun! We ______________ do what we wanted!
3 My family ______________ go on holiday. We were very sad.
4 ______________ you see the sea from the top of the mountain?

7 ★ Completa la regola del *present continuous* con valore di futuro.

definitivi programmi quando

Il *present continuous* si può usare per parlare di ¹ ______________ futuri, quando questi sono ² ______________ e sappiamo con precisione ³ ______________ e dove avranno luogo.

8 ★★ Completa le frasi con il *present continuous* dei verbi del riquadro.

~~come~~ go meet ride visit not / walk

Is Suzi coming (Suzi) to the leisure centre with us?

1 We ______________ in the library, on Saturday.
2 Harry ______________, he ______________ his bike to the park.
3 My class ______________ an art gallery next week.
4 ______________ (you) to the cinema tomorrow?

9 ★ Cerchia l'espressione di tempo al futuro corretta.

- ***this* / *in*** month, week, year
- ***tomorrow* / *this*** morning, afternoon, night
- ***in* / *next*** two weeks, 3 years, ten minutes
- ***next* / *tomorrow*** year, summer, Friday

10 ★ Completa la regola del *present simple* con valore di futuro.

momento eventi

Il *present simple* si può usare per parlare di ¹ ______________ futuri che si svolgeranno in un ² ______________ preciso e stabilito.

11 ★ Completa con i verbi del riquadro al *present simple*.

~~begin~~ finish leave start not / open

The autumn term begins on 3rd September.

1 My party ______________ at 10 pm!
2 The museum ______________ on Mondays.
3 The school holidays ______________ next week.
4 What time (the train) ______________ ?

Grammar Round-up

12 ★★ **Cerchia l'opzione corretta.**

The Roman Museum

Our new Roman Museum (is) / *was* a great new experience! Discover what your town was like two thousand years [1]*ago* / *past*!

Exchester [2]*is* / *was* an important Roman town. It [3]*has* / *had* many big buildings and a lot of people lived here. The museum [4]*shows* / *showed* you the lives of ordinary people: where they lived and [5]*work* / *worked*. You can also see what they [6]*do* / *did* in their free time. They didn't [7]*have* / *had* our modern games but you can [8]*see* / *saw* the games and sports they enjoyed.

The museum opens at 9.30 and [9]*closes* / *is closing* at 6 pm.

Special event [10]*next* / *last* week: we [11]*organise* / *are organising* a visit and workshop for school students next Saturday. The visit [12]*starts* / *start* at 9 am. Reserve your place on the museum website!

13 ★★★ **Completa con i verbi tra parentesi al *past simple* oppure al *present continuous* o *present simple* con valore di futuro.**

A What *are you doing* (do) this weekend, Lisa?
B I [1] ______________ (go) away with my family. We [2] ______________ (spend) two days in York.
A Lucky you! I [3] ______________ (go) there last year.
B [4] ______________ (you / like) it?
A It's a great place with a lot of history.
B What [5] ______________ (you / see)?
A We [6] ______________ (visit) the old town. We [7] ______________ (not / see) the new part.
B We [8] ______________ (travel) there by train.
A Good idea. It's a long way! I [9] ______________ (not / enjoy) the car journey!
B Yes, but our train [10] ______________ (leave) at 6 in the morning!

14 ★★★ **Scrivi le frasi usando i suggerimenti.**

next week / we / go / on holiday
Next week we're going on holiday.

1 they / not / go / sea / last summer
____
2 you / visit / London / next month?
____
3 the art gallery / open / at 2 pm / this afternoon
____
4 what / you / buy / at the bookshop / yesterday?
____
5 Toby / have / party / in two weeks!
____
6 Louise / work / in the hospital / last year?
____

15 ★★★ **Completa il testo con una parola per spazio.**

New message

To patrick@your_mail.co.uk
Subject Holidays!

Hi Patrick!

We*'re* going on holiday tomorrow!

We did [1] ______________ have a holiday last summer so I'm [2] ______________ excited!

We're flying to Greece [3] ______________ it's my first time on a plane! We arrive in Greece [4] ______________ 11.30 so we're going [5] ______________ the beach in the afternoon.

[6] ______________ you enjoy your trip to Spain?

Write soon,

Rory

Send

16 ★★★ **Scrivi le domande e poi rispondi.**

you / go / holiday / last year?
'Did you go on holiday last year?' 'Yes, I did.'

1 Where / stay?
____
2 Who / go with?
____
3 How / travel?
____
4 What / do?
____
5 be / good holiday?
____

Reading

Holiday adverts

1 BEFORE YOU READ Rispondi alle domande.

1 What's your favourite place for a holiday? Why?
2 What do you enjoy doing on holiday?

2 Leggi i volantini delle vacanze e indica (✓) se le frasi sono vere (T = *true*) o false (F = *false*). Poi correggi quelle false.

A Beach Fun

Enjoy five days of holiday fun at The Sea Shell holiday park. Families stay in comfortable holiday flats.

Fun activities for children 5-10 and teens 11-15.

Open from May to October!

B Winter Sun

Come to the Winter Sun resort in the mountains and try skiing, snowboarding and skating.

Lessons every day with our instructors special prices for families.

— From November to April —

C Hikers' Holiday

Spend a few days on Seahorse Island on a walking holiday. Walk through the forest, climb the rocks and relax on the beach.

Visitors stay in cabins in our forest camp.

Open all year!

D Europe by train!

Calling all backpackers!

Buy a two-week train ticket and visit the cities of Europe from Athens to Oslo and Madrid. It's easy! Special summer holiday prices for students.

E LAKE ADVENTURES

Water sports, camping and fun on Lake Kata. Lake Kata summer camp is in the mountains and open in spring and summer.

Climbing, canoeing and windsurfing lessons every day.

	T	F
1 All the holidays are in the summer.	☐	☐
2 The holidays are only for teenagers.	☐	☐

3 Leggi di nuovo i testi dell'es. 2 e abbina i volantini (A–E) alle frasi (1–6). Puoi usare un volantino più di una volta. La prima risposta (0) è un esempio. Ⓘ

0 _B_ This holiday is only in the winter.
1 ___ On this holiday you do a lot of winter sports.
2 ___ On this holiday you visit a lot of different places.
3 ___ On this holiday you stay on a camp-site.
4 ___ This holiday is a relaxing holiday by the sea.
5 ___ You arrive at this holiday place by boat.
6 ___ You can go on this holiday in all the seasons.

Holiday memories

4 BEFORE YOU READ Rispondi alle domande.

1 Do you like visiting museums? Why?
2 What was the last museum you visited?

5 Leggi il resoconto della visita al museo di Eddie e scegli la risposta corretta (A, B o C).

Eddie's blog

A Visit to a Living History Museum

A living history museum brings history to life.

The living history museum that we [1] ______ was a town with houses, shops, [2] ______ and transport just like 120 years ago. Visitors could go into the houses and look at the rooms and see how ordinary families [3] ______ in the past. The shops were original old buildings and they sold things to the visitors. We bought some [4] ______ from the baker's and some fruit from the [5] ______ for our picnic! We watched a show in the theatre. I also sent a postcard from the post office. The school was open too and you could go to a lesson – but I didn't [6] ______ to!

The trip on the river was fun, especially when the boat went through a long [7] ______ – that was scary!

1 **A** went	**B** visited	**C** travelled
2 **A** streets	**B** bridges	**C** corners
3 **A** stayed	**B** left	**C** lived
4 **A** ham	**B** bread	**C** lettuce
5 **A** chemist's	**B** florist's	**C** greengrocer's
6 **A** want	**B** wanted	**C** wants
7 **A** pavement	**B** tunnel	**C** roundabout

6 BEFORE YOU READ Rispondi alle domande.

1 Do you send postcards or photos of your holiday to your friends?
2 Do you like receiving postcards or photos of your friends' holidays? Why?

7 Leggi l'email di Grace e completa gli appunti (1–3).

8 Rileggi e completa l'email con una parola per spazio.

Place:
1 ______________

Staying in:
2 ______________

Activities:
3 ______________

New message

To sophie@your_mail.co.uk

Hi Sophie,

We're having a great holiday in Ireland. We [a] ______________ staying in a small house [b] ______________ the sea. Yesterday we visited an old castle – it [c] ______________ brilliant! Tomorrow, we're going to the beach all day! The beach looks lovely and I love swimming in the sea! Today, we're going into town because we need [d] ______________ shopping.

Tomorrow, we want to go on a boat trip [e] ______________ an island with a lot of sea birds. There are [f] ______________ cars on the island, so everybody walks!

See you soon,

Grace

Send

Listening and Writing

Listening

1 BEFORE YOU LISTEN Rispondi alle domande.

1 What big cities are there near where you live?
2 What do you like doing in a big city?

2 09 Ascolta un insegnante che racconta il programma di una gita alla classe e numera i luoghi nell'ordine in cui li senti nominare.

☐ art gallery
☐ bridge
☐ castle
1 hostel
☐ museum
☐ old town
☐ river

3 Osserva l'immagine nell'es. 4. Quanti e quali luoghi citati nell'es. 2 riesci a vedere?

4 10 Ascolta di nuovo. Durante l'ascolto, abbina i giorni della settimana (1–5) alle attività (A–H). Ci sono due attività in più. La prima risposta (0) è un esempio. Ascolterai la registrazione due volte.

0 _H_ Saturday
1 ___ Sunday
2 ___ Monday
3 ___ Tuesday
4 ___ Wednesday
5 ___ Thursday

A art gallery
B museum
C sightseeing
D stadium
E cycling trip
F leisure centre
G castle
H theatre

5 BEFORE YOU LISTEN Rispondi alle domande.

1 Do you like shopping? Why / Why not?

2 Where does your family usually go shopping?

6 🔊 11 Ascolta Ethan che parla con la sua amica Milly di una gita e indica (✓) il riassunto corretto.

1 ☐ Milly and Ethan are going to scout camp in the mountains. They decide to go shopping to buy the things they need for the trip. Milly doesn't enjoy shopping.

2 ☐ Milly is surprised to meet Ethan in town. Ethan is going to scout camp and needs to buy some things. She tells him which shops to go to but then decides to go shopping with him.

7 🔊 11 Ascolta di nuovo e indica (✓) la risposta corretta (A, B o C).

1 Where do the friends meet?
- A ☐ On a beach.
- B ☐ In a town centre.
- C ☐ On a camp-site

2 Ethan is going away for … .
- A ☐ a long holiday
- B ☐ a week-end trip
- C ☐ just one day

3 He wants to buy … .
- A ☐ a swimsuit
- B ☐ flip flops
- C ☐ a backpack

4 What does Milly do?
- A ☐ Take him to the shop.
- B ☐ Show him a map.
- C ☐ Write him a list.

5 Milly knows a good shop for … .
- A ☐ clothes
- B ☐ shoes
- C ☐ things for the beach

Writing

8 Leggi la traccia con attenzione e scrivi la storia.

Look at the pictures.
Write the story shown in the pictures.
Write 35 words or more.

1

2

3

Vocabulary Review

Transport

1 ★☆☆ Scrivi i mezzi di trasporto del riquadro nella categoria corretta.

camper van ~~plane~~ boat motorbike helicopter coach bike train underground jeep scooter car cable car ship taxi ferry bus

Vehicles which ...

1 go in the air *plane* ______ ______

2 go on water ______ ______ ______

3 have two wheels ______ ______ ______

4 have four wheels ______ ______ ______ ______ ______

5 carry a lot of people ______ ______ ______ ______

2 ★☆☆ Abbina le due colonne per trovare mezzi di trasporto.

1 *C* cable	A scooter
2 ___ camper	B bike
3 ___ electric	C car
4 ___ motor	D van

3 ★★☆ Cerchia l'intruso.

	lorry	(boat)	coach	car
1	plane	cable car	helicopter	tram
2	scooter	moped	taxi	bike
3	train	underground	tram	jeep
4	ferry	van	ship	boat

4 ★★☆ Cancella la parola che non puoi usare con il verbo.

miss: a bus a train ~~a moped~~

1 **ride**: a motorbike a ferry a scooter

2 **catch**: a van a tram an underground train

3 **get on / get off**: a bus a jeep a train

4 **get into / get out of**: a car a taxi a coach

Jobs around the house

5 ★☆☆ Completa i lavori domestici con i verbi del riquadro.

~~do~~ do feed go lay / clear load / unload make put out tidy

do the cooking

1 ______ the pets

2 ______ food shopping

3 ______ the table

4 ______ the dishwasher

5 ______ your bed

6 ______ the rubbish

7 ______ your bedroom

8 ______ the vacuuming

6 ★☆☆ Completa i nomi degli strumenti di pulizia.

B *R* O *O* *M*

1 C __ E __ N __ R

2 C L __ T __

3 D __ S __ E __

4 __ U __ T P A _ N

5 M __ P

6 S P __ N G __

7 R __ __ __ E __ __ L __ __ __ S

7 ★☆☆ Scrivi i nomi degli strumenti di pulizia e degli elettrodomestici sotto le immagini.

vacuum cleaner

1 ______

2 ______

3 ______

Vocabulary Round-up

8 ★ **Trova l'anagramma e scrivilo sotto l'immagine corretta.**

pmo ~~obrom~~ nva ooscert ongeps
ryref ahocc renlcae otlch

broom

1 ____________

2 ____________

3 ____________

4 ____________

5 ____________

6 ____________

7 ____________

8 ____________

9 ★★ **Completa le definizioni.**

A *plane* flies all over the world.

1 A ____________ washes dirty clothes.
2 An ____________ has two small wheels and an electric motor.
3 A ____________ is a small lorry. It transports things.
4 A ____________ is a machine to clean the floor.
5 A ____________ has two wheels, an engine and it goes fast.
6 A ____________ is for holidays. You drive it and live in it.
7 A ____________ is where we put old things, like paper, we don't need.
8 A ____________ hangs from cables and takes people up mountains.
9 A ____________ takes people across water between two places.
10 A ____________ cleans dirty plates, cups and glasses.

10 ★★ **Completa il testo con le parole del riquadro.**

catch getting into get off get on
~~getting out~~ missed car helicopter
lorry underground riding

I live in the town centre and it's a very busy day today. From my window I can see a woman *getting out* of a taxi and walking into the station. Now a man is [1] ____________ the taxi. I can hear a [2] ____________. It's flying to the hospital, I think.
Some people are [3] ____________ their bikes and other people are going down to the [4] ____________ station.
A small group of people are at the bus stop. They're waiting to [5] ____________ a bus. Oh, now the bus is there! First some school kids [6] ____________ the bus and then the other people [7] ____________ it and it leaves. A girl is running to the bus stop – but she [8] ____________ the bus! I can see a big [9] ____________ too. It's full of things for the shops. Oh look, now there's a police [10] ____________ outside the station.
This is getting exciting!

11 ★★★ **Scrivi in quale lavoro domestico è impegnato ciascun membro della famiglia.**

Granny is in the garden. She's putting the wet clothes to dry. She's *hanging out the washing*.

1 Dad is at the supermarket. He's buying the food for the week. He's ____________.
2 Mum is using a machine to clean all the floors in the house. She's ____________.
3 Matthew's in the kitchen. He's taking the clean plates and cups out of a machine and putting them in the cupboards.
He's ____________.
4 Amanda's in the kitchen too. She's making lunch for all the family.
She's ____________.
5 Emily loves animals. She's giving some food to their dog and cat.
She's ____________.

Grammar Review

1 ★ **Completa le regole sul comparativo di maggioranza degli aggettivi regolari.**

Agli aggettivi regolari si aggiunge : *-er*
old → [1] ______

Ricorda:

- Aggettivi + raddoppio della consonante + *-er*: *hot* → [2] ______
- Aggettivi + *-r*: *brave* → [3] ______
- Aggettivi – *-y* + *-ier*: *dirty* → [4] ______
- Aggettivi con due o più sillabe: *more* + aggettivo: *interesting* → [5] ______

2 ★ **Completa con il comparativo di maggioranza dell'aggettivo tra parentesi.**

You were *later* (late) than me this morning.

1 My room is ______ (tidy) than my brother's.
2 This match is ______ (exciting) than the last one.
3 Emma's phone is ______ (new) than mine.
4 I think blue is ______ (nice) than green.

3 ★ **Abbina gli aggettivi irregolari ai relativi comparativi di maggioranza.**

1 ___ good
2 ___ bad
3 ___ far

A worse
B farther
C better

4 ★★ **Scrivi le frasi usando il comparativo di maggioranza e i suggerimenti.**

I think / trains / cars (good)
I think trains are better than cars.

1 London / Paris (far)
2 The science test / the English test (bad)
3 Motorbikes / cars (good)
4 Your house / my house (far from our school)

5 ★★ **Scrivi le frasi usando i suggerimenti e *as … as* / *not as … as*.**

Jack is 1.3 m / Sarah is 1.5 m (tall)
Jack *isn't as tall as Sarah* .

1 Lucy is 13 / Harry is 13 (old)
Lucy ______________________ .
2 Water is £1 / Apple juice is £1.10 (expensive)
Water ______________________ .
3 My flat has five rooms / Your house has six rooms (big)
My flat ______________________ .

6 ★ **Completa con il superlativo relativo degli aggettivi tra parentesi.**

That was *the most difficult* (difficult) test!

1 My bike is ______________ (fast).
2 Our classroom is ______________ (big).
3 Tigers are ______________ (good) team.
4 It was ______________ (interesting) lesson ever!

7 ★ **Completa la regola su *one* / *ones*.**

Per sostituire i sostantivi singolari si usa [1] ______ ,
per sostituire i sostantivi plurali si usa [2] ______ .

8 ★ **Cerchia l'opzione corretta: *one* o *ones*.**

Do you want a red pen or a blue (*one*) / *ones*?

1 Which cars do you like? Fast *one* / *ones*.
2 Is this your umbrella. No, that *one* / *ones* is mine.
3 Which sandwiches are mine?
The cheese *one* / *ones*.
4 Did you use your new bike or your old *one* / *ones*?

9 ★★ **Scrivi le frasi usando i suggerimenti e la forma corretta di *have to*.**

Matt / make his bed / every morning.
Matt has to make his bed every morning.

1 We / wash the car / last week.
2 you / clear the table / every day?
3 they / do a lot of homework / yesterday?
4 Kate / never / help at home.
5 Jack / buy a bus ticket?
6 The children / not / travel by bus.

10 ★ **Abbina le frasi per scrivere le regole su *must* / *mustn't* / *don't have to*.**

1 ___ *must* si usa per indicare
2 ___ *mustn't* si usa per indicare
3 ___ *don't have to* si usa per indicare

A un divieto.
B che non è obbligatorio fare una certa cosa.
C un ordine.

11 ★ **Le azioni sono obbligatorie (O = *obligation*), vietate (P = *prohibition*) o non necessarie (N = *not necessary*)?**

O *Shh.* You must be quiet!

1 ___ You don't have to pay.
2 ___ You mustn't run in the corridor!
3 ___ We must clean the classroom after Art lessons.
4 ___ They must tell the teacher – it's important.

Grammar Round-up

12 ★★★ Scegli la risposta corretta (A, B o C).

A Did you have a good day at the lake?

B Not bad. We walked ten kilometres.

A You ___ to walk ten kilometres! That's [1]___ than I can walk!

B It was my [2]___ walk and the [3]___ difficult because it was up and down the hills.

A That's not for me!

B Anyway we visited the castle – it's [4]___ oldest one in the area.

A [5]___ you have to walk back?

B No, the trip back was the [6]___ thing. The plan was to get the boat but we missed the last [7]______! Luckily there was a train.

A That was OK then.

B Except we had [8]___ run to the station!

A You [9]___ plan your trips [10]___ next time!

	A	B	C
	A have	**(B)** had	**C** has
1	**A** far	**B** farthest	**C** farther
2	**A** longest	**B** longer	**C** long
3	**A** more	**B** most	**C** very
4	**A** the	**B** than	**C** an
5	**A** Must	**B** Do	**C** Did
6	**A** bad	**B** worst	**C** most
7	**A** one	**B** it	**C** two
8	**A** to	**B** at	**C** in
9	**A** have	**B** mustn't	**C** must
10	**A** good	**B** better	**C** worse

13 ★★★ Cerchia l'opzione corretta.

There are six people in my family, so there ***is*** / (***are***) a lot of jobs to do round the house. Before it was terrible: my sisters and brother never [1]***wanted to*** / ***wanted*** help so Mum and Dad were often angry. I decided this [2]***had*** / ***must*** to change. My brother wasn't happy because his best friend [3]***don't*** / ***doesn't*** have to help at home at all. My sisters always clean their room but they [4]***must*** / ***had*** to do more.

Every week, I make a plan with the jobs for each person. For example, on Tuesday, I [5]***must*** / ***mustn't*** feed the dog, my brother [6]***has got*** / ***has to*** put out the rubbish and my sisters [7]***have*** / ***has*** to clear and lay the table.

Now, we are a [8]***happier*** / ***more happy*** family! Mum and Dad [9]***don't have to*** / ***mustn't*** do all the jobs. All my family say I found the [10]***better*** / ***best*** solution to the problem!

14 ★★★ Completa la seconda frase in modo che abbia lo stesso significato della prima.

It isn't necessary to catch a bus.

We *don't have to* to catch a bus.

1. Kim is tall but Lenny is taller.
   Lenny is ______________________ Kim.
2. We feed our cat every day. It's very important.
   We ______________________ our cat every day.
3. Dad's got all the food. We don't need to go shopping.
   We ______________________ to go shopping.
4. History is difficult for me but Maths is easy.
   I think Maths is ______________________ than History.
5. Cycling is fast, walking is slow.
   Cycling is ______________________ than walking.
6. Dan broke his leg and he has to rest.
   Dan ______________________ walk or run.

15 ★★★ Completa il testo con una parola per spazio.

What's the best way to travel? That's a difficult question *because* now we have to think about our planet too.

I think going by bike or [1]____________ foot are [2]____________ healthiest ways for us to travel. [3]____________ are also good for the planet! We [4]____________ try to walk and cycle more.

Public transport, like trains, are better [5]____________ cars because a lot of passengers travel in one vehicle. But many people prefer cars and motorbikes because they can go [6]____________ they like, when they like.

Transport [7]____________ changing for the future – there are already [8]____________ electric cars and scooters on the roads than a few years ago.

16 ★★★ Scrivi le domande e poi rispondi.

What / your / favourite way / travelling?

What's your favourite way of travelling?

1. How often / you / travel / car?
2. What / your / longest trip?
3. How / you / travel / school?
4. Which jobs / you / do / around the house?
5. What / the worst job?
6. Which / jobs / you / like?

Reading

A trip to London

1 BEFORE YOU READ Rispondi alle domande.

1 What do enjoy visiting in a big city?
2 What's the best way to travel round a city?

2 Leggi le informazioni sulle gite da fare in una giornata a Londra e abbina le due metà di ogni frase.

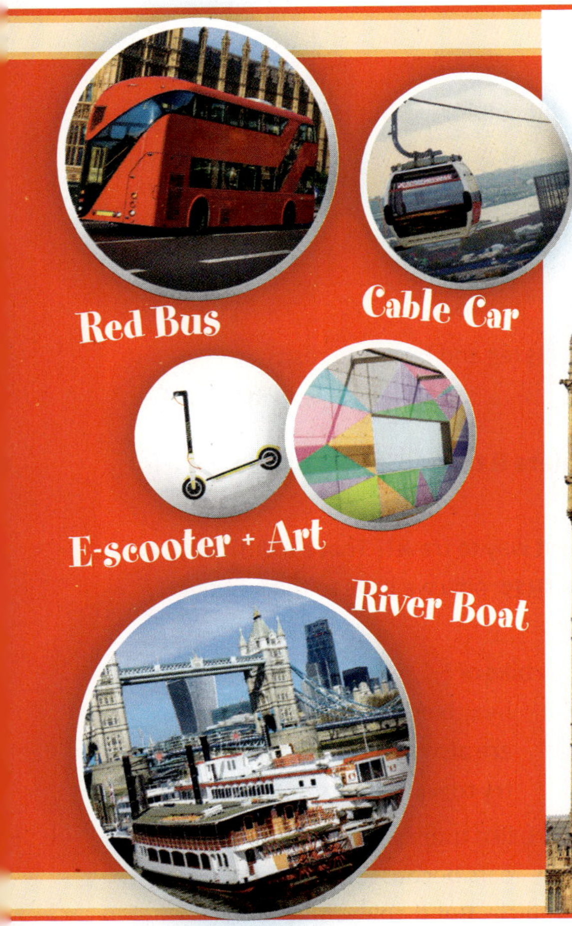

VISIT LONDON!

Make your visit to London more exciting!
Try one of our day trips!

Cable Car

Go to Greenwich or the Royal Docks to catch the cable car across the River Thames.
The trip takes 5–13 minutes, depending on the weather.
Tickets: £8 for adults and £4 for children.
Opening times: from 7.00 am to 10 am most days, check our website for the latest times.

E-scooter + Art

You must see London's Street Art!
Rent an electric scooter and download the Scooterart app to book your scooter and get maps and information.
Prices start from £30.

River Boat

Take a relaxing boat trip along the River Thames from Westminster to The Tower of London. Look and listen to the history of London.
Drinks and snacks available on board.
Tickets from £13 – you don't have to book!

Red Bus

The best way to see London is from the top of a Red Bus!
Day tickets for central London: £25 a person.
Get on and get off the bus when and where you like! Or, just stray on the bus and enjoy a sightseeing tour!

	C	The cable car trip	A	you hear some stories.
1	___	You use the e-scooter	B	for 24 hours.
2	___	On the boat trip,	C	crosses a river.
3	___	You can use your Red Bus ticket	D	to see pictures outdoors.

3 Leggi di nuovo le informazioni e indica (✓) se le affermazioni (1–6) sono vere (T = *true*), false (F = *false*) o se la risposta non è deducibile dal testo (NG = *not given*). La prima risposta (0) è un esempio.

		T	F	NG
0	The cable car trip is short.	✓		
1	Children's cable car tickets are more expensive than adults' ones.			
2	You have to return your scooter after one hour.			
3	The cheapest e-scooter + art tickets cost £30.			
4	You must not eat on the River Boat trip.			
5	You must buy tickets for the boat the day before your trip.			
6	The Red Bus travels around the city centre.			

What do you have to do?

4 BEFORE YOU READ Osserva i testi (1–6) dell'es. 5 e abbina ogni testo alla sua descrizione.

~~text message~~ advert for sale card note shopping list sign

1 *text message*
2 ______
3 ______
4 ______
5 ______
6 ______

5 Leggi i testi (1–6) e rispondi alle domande.

1

Lisa

In the morning, I can catch the bus at 10.15 or an hour later. In the evening, my last bus home leaves at 6.30 pm. Let me know which is best for you. Jo

2

PASSENGERS MUST GET ON THE BUS AT THE FRONT AND GET OFF AT THE BACK.

3

Tom and Kate,
I have to work late today. Can you please lay the table for dinner and feed the pets?
Thanks,
Mum

4

- Rubber gloves
- A bottle of cleaner
- Sponge

5

BIKE FOR SALE
Mountain bike
(for boy or girl).
Only 2 years' old.
Good condition but needs cleaning.
Contact: Marty on 765 3399549 after 5 pm.

6

This week only:
20% off
all dishwashers
and washing
machines.
Free broom for all customers!

Which text (1–6)

is about selling one thing? 5
1 tells someone what they must do? ___
2 is about things you must buy? ___
3 asks for information? ___
4 gives instructions to passengers? ___
5 is about special offers in a shop? ___

6 Leggi di nuovo i testi (1–6) dell'es. 5 e indica (✓) la risposta corretta.

1 What does Jo want to know?
A ☐ The times of the buses.
B ☐ Which bus to catch.
C ☐ Where to meet Lisa.

2 What does text 2 mean?
A ☐ You mustn't get on the bus at the back.
B ☐ You can't get on the bus without a ticket.
C ☐ You can use both doors to get off the bus.

3 Tom and Kate have to … .
A ☐ do the cooking
B ☐ do the shopping
C ☐ do some extra jobs

4 Read text 4 again. What job does Max have to do?
A ☐ cooking
B ☐ ironing
C ☐ wash the car

5 The bike is … .
A ☐ for a young child
B ☐ works well but is dirty
C ☐ very expensive

6 What does text 6 mean?
A ☐ Brooms are 20% cheaper.
B ☐ Dishwashers are cheaper than washing machines.
C ☐ Customers pay less for some cleaning equipment.

7–8

Listening and Writing

Listening

1 BEFORE YOU LISTEN Osserva le immagini delle domande (1–5) dell'es. 3 e abbinale alle categorie (A–G). Ci sono due categorie in più.

Pictures

1 B
2 ___
3 ___
4 ___
5 ___

Words

A parts of a house
B jobs at home
C prices
D shopping
E travel
F vehicle
G washing

2 12 Ascolta i cinque mini-dialoghi e numera le parole nell'ordine in cui le senti.

☐ train ☐ bedroom ☐ garage ☐ blue ☐ house

3 12 Ascolta di nuovo e indica (✓) la risposta corretta (A, B o C).

1 What does the boy have to do?

A ☐

B ☐

C ☐

2 How is the girl travelling to her friend's house?

A ☐

B ☐

C ☐

3 Where is the rubbish bin?

A ☐

B ☐

C ☐

4 How much does the ticket cost now?

A ☐

B ☐

C ☐

5 Which is the girl's scooter?

A ☐

B ☐

C ☐

4 BEFORE YOU LISTEN Rispondi alle domande.

1 How do you travel to school?
2 How long does it take you?

5 🔊 13 Ascolta Isabel che parla di quale mezzo di trasporto usa per andare a scuola. Indica (✓) i mezzi di trasporto che senti.

- [ ] bike
- [ ] boat
- [ ] bus
- [ ] coach
- [ ] ferry
- [ ] on foot
- [ ] taxi

6 🔊 14 Ascolta di nuovo. Durante l'ascolto, rispondi alle domande (1–5). Usa quattro parole al massimo. La prima risposta (0) è un esempio. Ascolterai la registrazione due volte. Ⓘ

0 Where does Isabel live?
On an island.
1 Where is her school? ____________
2 How many students travel with her? ____________
3 How do they travel? ____________
4 How long is the trip across the sea? ____________
5 Why can't she get to school sometimes? ____________

Writing

7 Leggi la traccia con attenzione e scrivi l'email.

Your English friend, Joe, wants to know about your journey to school every day.
Write an email to Joe.
In the email:

- describe your journey to school
- say what you like and don't like about it
- ask Joe to tell you how he travels to school

Write 25 words or more.

Oracy

Oracy

Oracy Introduction

CHE COS'È L'ORACY? È La nostra capacità di esprimerci in maniera adeguata e comunicare con gli altri con successo, come ad esempio fare una presentazione, partecipare attivamente a un dibattito o a una discussione di gruppo o a un'attività di tipo collaborativo, è la nostra abilità di persuadere gli altri, di ascoltare in modo attivo, di facilitare le decisioni condivise.
Questa sezione del libro è dedicata a un aspetto specifico dell'*Oracy*: come fare una presentazione orale. Troverai quindi consigli e strategie per prepararti a sostenere un orale, e anche il colloquio durante l'Esame di Stato.

Quando si parla di *Oracy*, sono 4 le aree su cui è importante concentrarsi:

1. **area fisico-motoria**: come usare la voce e il linguaggio del corpo
2. **area linguistica**: come scegliere le parole da utilizzare
3. **area cognitiva**: come strutturare le nostre idee e argomentarle
4. **area socio-emotiva**: come rapportarsi con noi stessi e con gli altri

Vediamo come possono esserti utili per preparare una presentazione orale.

1 Area fisico-motoria

- Controllare la voce
- Controllare postura e linguaggio del corpo

Durante una presentazione è importante capire come usare la voce e il proprio corpo.

Ricorda e controlla:

- Com'è il tono di voce? (ad es., basso o acuto?)
- Che cosa esprimi con il corpo? (ad es., hai le braccia incrociate?)
- Il tuo viso è espressivo? (ad es., stai sorridendo?)

Trovi qui la **Presentation skill** per prepararti:
- **Mostrare immagini e oggetti** p. 44

COME FARE UNA PRESENTAZIONE ORALE

2 Area linguistica

- Scegliere un lessico adeguato
- Utilizzare la grammatica in modo corretto

Quando fai una presentazione è essenziale saper scegliere le parole da utilizzare e strutturare le frasi in modo corretto.

Ricorda e controlla:

- Con chi stai parlando? (ad es., a un docente o agli amici?)
- Di che cosa e perché? (ad es., le parole che usi sono corrette?)

Trovi qui la **Presentation skill** per prepararti:
- **Usare varietà lessicale** p. 42

3 Area cognitiva

- Organizzare i contenuti
- Ragionare, chiarire, sintetizzare
- Fornire argomentazioni

Per poter presentare oralmente un argomento devi prima organizzare i contenuti in maniera chiara e logica, e poi saperne discutere.

Ricorda e controlla:

- Si capisce che cosa stai dicendo?
- Come puoi chiarire meglio?
- Il tuo discorso segue un filo logico?
- Sai motivare le tue opinioni?

Trovi qui la **Presentation skill** per prepararti:

- **Mettere le informazioni in ordine** **p. 40**

4 Area socio-emotiva

- Parlare con naturalezza
- Ascoltare in modo attivo e rispondere in modo appropriato

È importante, durante una presentazione, esporre in maniera scorrevole e vivace, percepire se chi ti ascolta sta seguendo il tuo discorso e intervenire prontamente in caso di domande.

Ricorda e controlla:

- Ti senti a tuo agio?
- Sei coinvolgente?
- Sei consapevole di ciò che succede intorno a te, tra chi ti ascolta? (ad es., il tuo pubblico si annoia o sembra confuso?)

Trovi qui la **Presentation skill** per prepararti:

- **Essere preparati a rispondere a domande** **p. 46**

Oracy Oral presentation A

Prepare

1 15 **Leggi e ascolta la presentazione.**

Cheese and Tomato Toastie

My favourite sandwich is a cheese and tomato toastie. I like it because it's hot and it's quick and easy to make! It's perfect for Saturday lunch when I'm hungry after my swimming lesson.

These are the ingredients you need:

- Two slices of bread
- 1 or 2 tomatoes
- Slices of your favourite cheese

Now, this is how you make it:

- Put one slice of bread on a plate. First, put some cheese on the bread.
- Then, cut the tomato and put it on the cheese. Next, cover the tomato with more cheese. Finally put the other slice of bread on top.
- Put it under a hot grill for a few minutes, then turn it and grill the other side.
- Finally, cut the sandwich in two and put it on a plate. Eat it immediately. Enjoy!

Glossary: toastie toasted sandwich

Area cognitiva

Presentation SKILL

Mettere le informazioni in ordine

Quando prepari una presentazione orale, organizza sempre le informazioni in ordine logico.

2 Rileggi la presentazione e indica (✓) se le frasi sono vere (T = *true*) o false (F = *false*).

	T	F
1 This sandwich takes a long time to make.	☐	☐
2 It's a good snack when you are hungry.	☐	☐
3 It needs a lot of ingredients.	☐	☐
4 You cook it for a short time.	☐	☐

3 Rileggi la presentazione e numera i titoli in base all'ordine in cui le informazioni compaiono nel testo.

___ Ingredients
___ How to serve
___ Why I like this sandwich
___ Instructions on how to make it

TIPS

Esporre in sequenza

Durante la presentazione orale, usa le seguenti parole per descrivere una serie di azioni in sequenza:

- *First, Second, Third*
- *First, Then, Next, Finally*

4 Rileggi il terzo paragrafo della presentazione che spiega come fare il *cheese and tomato toastie*. Quali parole sono state usate per indicare l'ordine delle azioni da seguire? Completa la sequenza.

1 First
2 ______
3 ______
4 Finally

Research, plan and write

5 Scegli una ricetta semplice per uno snack o una bevanda. Cerca le istruzioni per farla.

6 Scrivi il nome dello snack o della bevanda al centro della mappa. Poi completala con le tue idee. Trova un'immagine del piatto pronto.

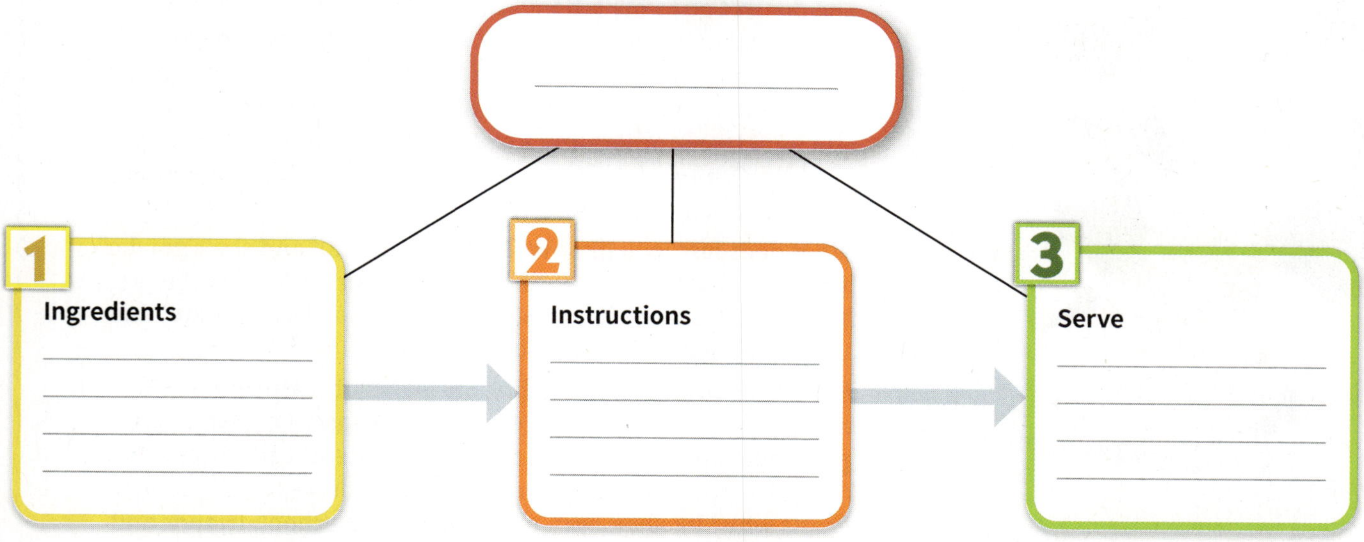

7 Ora sfrutta gli appunti presi nell'es. 6 per scrivere ciò che vuoi esporre nella tua presentazione orale. Usa il testo dell'es. 1 come modello e i box *Presentation skill* e *Tips*. Aggiungi l'immagine scelta.

Speaking: Practise and present

8 Prova a leggere la presentazione ad alta voce più volte, poi registrala o fanne un video.

Evaluate

9 Ascolta / Guarda la registrazione della presentazione orale e rispondi alle domande.

1 What did you do well?
2 What do you need to improve?
3 How well was the *Presentation skill* used? Tick (✓) the symbol.

10 Leggi il box 3 Area cognitiva a pagina 39 e rispondi alle domande scegliendo il simbolo più appropriato.

1 Was your oral presentation clear enough?
2 Was your oral presentation well planned?
3 Did you say why you like the snack / drink in your presentation?

Oracy Oral presentation B

Prepare

1 16 **Leggi e ascolta la presentazione.**

MY FRIEND JESS

by Grace

I've got friends at school and at home but my special friend is Jess.

She doesn't go to my school but she lives near me. I met her on the first day at dance classes. She was new too, and we immediately made friends! I see Jess every week at the dance school and we sometimes meet after school or at weekends. She's got two brothers and a sister and her family are all very friendly. Our two families often go out and do things together because we enjoy the same things.

What does Jess look like? Well, she's quite tall and she's got dark hair – it's short and wavy. She had long hair before but she prefers it short now. I think her new hairstyle is cool. Her eyes are blue and she's got a few freckles on her nose.

Jess has got a great personality. She's usually calm and hardly ever gets worried. I think she's clever because she always has good ideas and knows what to do in all different situations. But, she's also funny and very kind to her friends, especially to me. That's why I like her. I can talk to her about school, friends and everything because she understands me. Like all of us, she isn't perfect. She occasionally gets angry – especially with her sister – and sometimes she's a bit quiet and serious.

Jess is a special person and I think I'm lucky she's my friend.

2 Rileggi la presentazione e rispondi alle domande.

1. How did Grace meet her friend?
2. What does Jess look like?
3. What's her personality like?
4. Why is Jess a special friend to Grace?

3 Rileggi il secondo e il terzo paragrafo e sottolinea tutti gli aggettivi.

4 Leggi e sostituisci le parole sottolineate (1–3) con le parole del riquadro.

cool ~~good~~ friendly long and wavy

My friend George is very nice. He is a ~~nice~~ friend **(A)** __ . good
He's tall and he's got green eyes and his hair is very [1] nice . **1** ________
(B) __ he's never angry, he's always [2] nice to me. **2** ________
His clothes are always [3] nice too. **(C)** __ . **3** ________

Area linguistica

Presentation SKILL

Usare varietà lessicale

Quando esponi una presentazione orale, fai attenzione a non ripetere sempre le stesse parole. Usa una scelta di parole differenti.

TIPS

Motivare le proprie opinioni

Quando esprimi un'opinione su qualcuno o qualcosa durante una presentazione orale, chiarisci sempre il motivo e fornisci delle argomentazioni.

5 Rileggi il terzo paragrafo della presentazione. Poi sottolinea e riscrivi i quattro esempi in cui Grace chiarisce le proprie opinioni.

I think she's clever because she always has good ideas ...

1 ______
2 ______
3 ______

6 Rileggi il testo dell'es. 4 e completa gli spazi (A–C) con le frasi corrette (1–3).

1 I like him because ...
2 ... because he's clever and funny.
3 We always have fun together.

Research, plan and write

7 Scegli un'amica o un amico di cui parlare.

8 Scrivi il nome dell'amica o dell'amico al centro della mappa. Poi completala con le tue idee. Trova un'immagine della tua amica o del tuo amico.

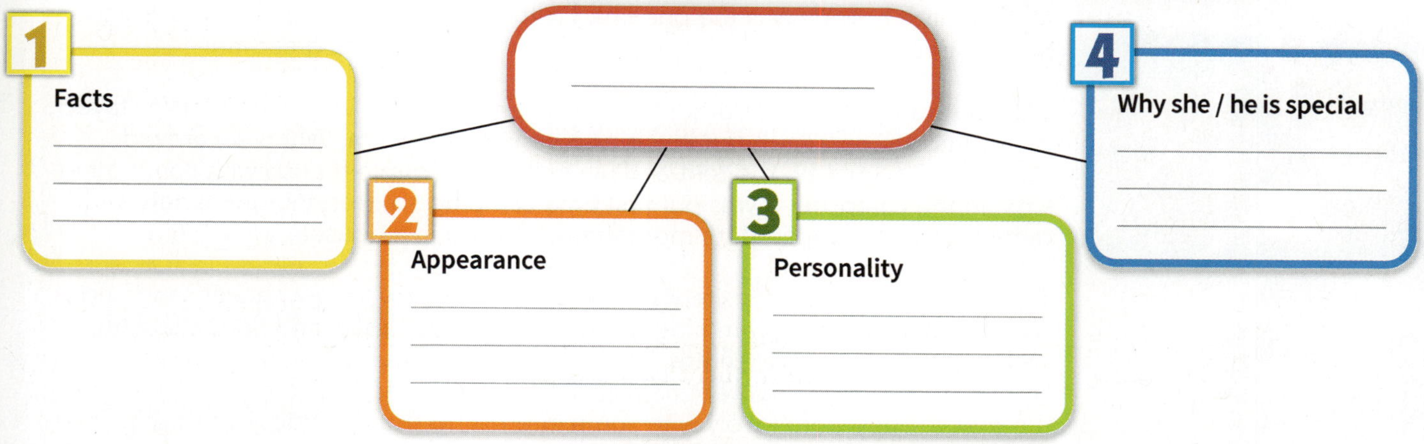

9 Ora sfrutta gli appunti presi nell'es. 8 per scrivere ciò che vuoi esporre nella tua presentazione orale. Usa il testo dell'es. 1 come modello e i box *Presentation skill* e *Tips*. Aggiungi l'immagine scelta.

Speaking: Practise and present

10 Prova a leggere la presentazione ad alta voce più volte, poi registrala o fanne un video.

Evaluate

11 Ascolta / Guarda la registrazione della presentazione orale e rispondi alle domande.

1 What did you do well?
2 What do you need to improve?
3 How well was the *Presentation skill* used? Tick (✓) the symbol.

12 Leggi il box 2 Area Linguistica a pagina 38 e rispondi alle domande scegliendo la risposta più appropriata.

1 Did you use formal or informal language? Why? ☐ formal ☐ informal
2 Did you use a lot of different words or repeat the same ones? ☐ different words ☐ same words
3 How correct was your grammar?

Oracy | Oral presentation C

Prepare

1 17 **Leggi e ascolta la presentazione.**

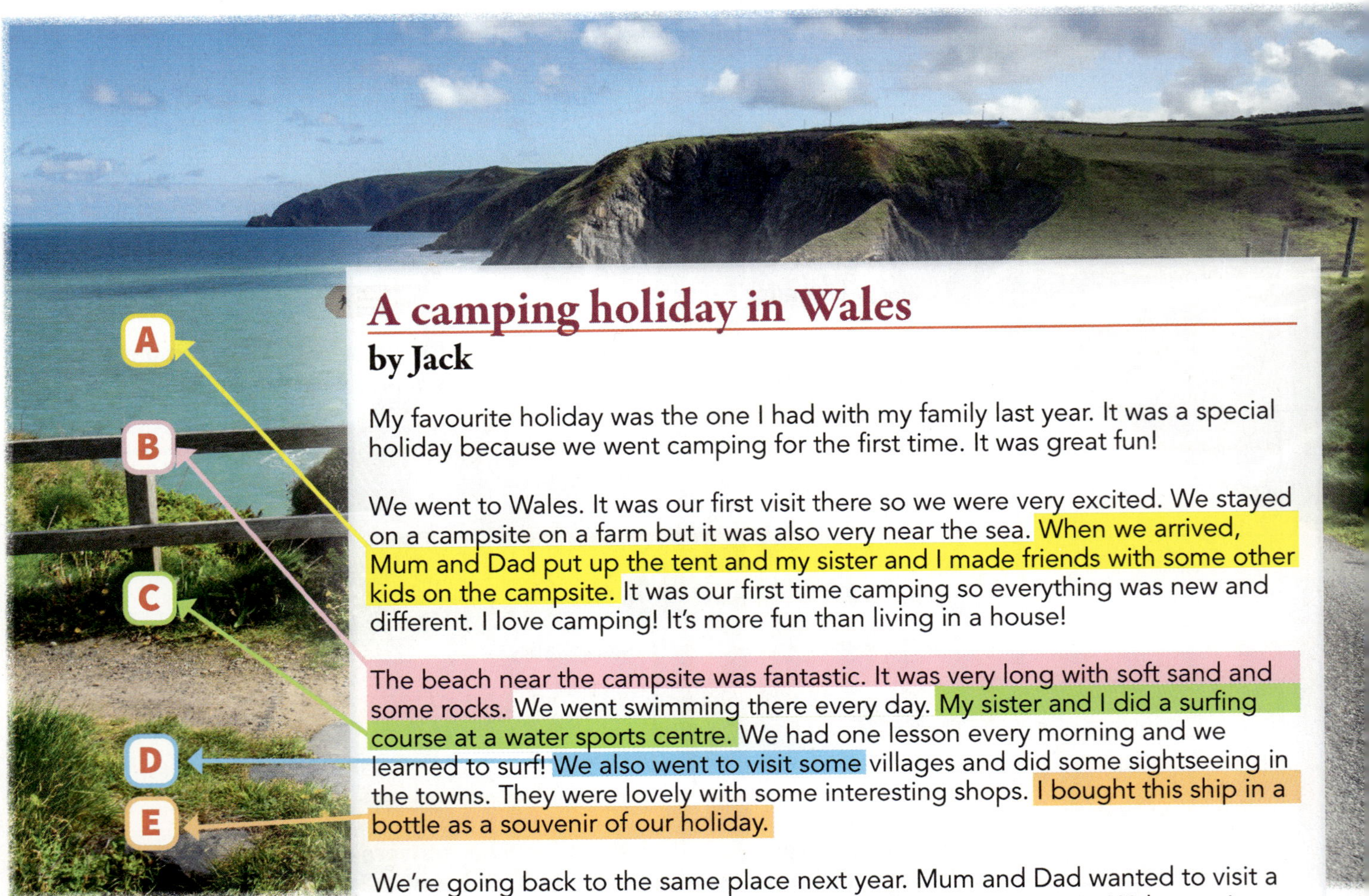

A camping holiday in Wales
by Jack

My favourite holiday was the one I had with my family last year. It was a special holiday because we went camping for the first time. It was great fun!

We went to Wales. It was our first visit there so we were very excited. We stayed on a campsite on a farm but it was also very near the sea. When we arrived, Mum and Dad put up the tent and my sister and I made friends with some other kids on the campsite. It was our first time camping so everything was new and different. I love camping! It's more fun than living in a house!

The beach near the campsite was fantastic. It was very long with soft sand and some rocks. We went swimming there every day. My sister and I did a surfing course at a water sports centre. We had one lesson every morning and we learned to surf! We also went to visit some villages and did some sightseeing in the towns. They were lovely with some interesting shops. I bought this ship in a bottle as a souvenir of our holiday.

We're going back to the same place next year. Mum and Dad wanted to visit a new place but my sister and I said we wanted to go camping in Wales again. I can't wait!

2 **Rileggi la presentazione e completa con le informazioni.**

Country:	Wales
When:	1 ________
Type of holiday:	2 ________
Activities:	3 ________
Souvenir:	4 ________

Area fisico-motoria

Presentation SKILL

Mostrare immagini e oggetti

Mentre fai la tua presentazione orale è importante renderla interessante, ad esempio mostrando immagini o oggetti di cui stai parlando.

3 **Jack ha alcune immagini e un oggetto da mostrare durante la presentazione. Abbina le frasi (1–5) alle frasi evidenziate nel testo (A–E).**

1 ___ This me surfing!
2 ___ We visited this village.
3 ___ This is the souvenir of my holiday.
4 ___ Here's a photo of our tent.
5 ___ This is the beach near the campsite.

TIPS

Usare i tempi presenti, passati e futuri

Durante la presentazione orale ricordati di usare correttamente i tempi verbali: presente, passato e futuro.

4 **Rileggi la presentazione e sottolinea i verbi al:**
- *Present simple*
- *Present continuous for future*
- *Past simple*

Research, plan and write

5 **Scegli la tua vacanza preferita.**

6 **Scrivi il nome della località al centro della mappa. Poi completala con le tue idee. Trova alcune immagini della vacanza e un souvenir, se lo hai.**

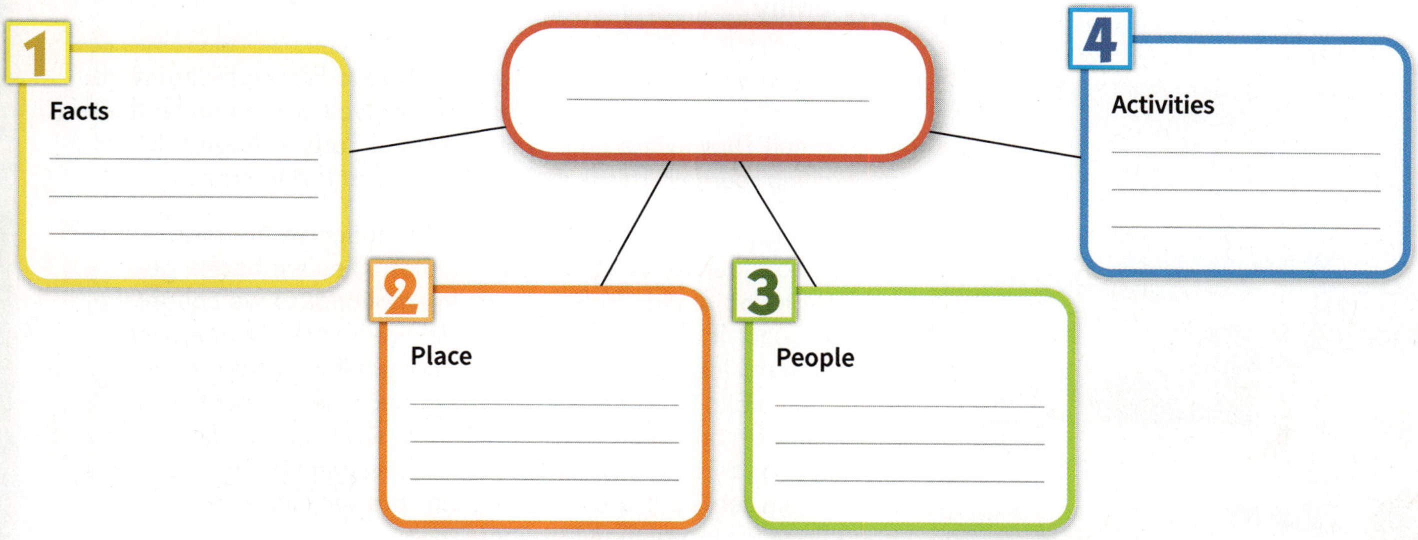

7 **Ora sfrutta gli appunti presi nell'es. 6 per scrivere ciò che vuoi esporre nella tua presentazione orale. Usa il testo dell'es. 1 come modello e i box *Presentation skill* e *Tips*. Decidi quando e come inserire le immagini e l'oggetto da mostrare.**

Speaking: Practise and present

8 **Prova a leggere la presentazione ad alta voce più volte, poi registrala o fanne un video.**

Evaluate

9 **Ascolta / Guarda la registrazione della presentazione orale e rispondi alle domande.**

1 What did you do well?
2 What do you need to improve?
3 How well was the *Presentation skill* used? Tick (✓) the symbol. 🙂 😐 🙁

10 **Leggi il box 1 Area fisico-motoria a pagina 38 e rispondi alle domande scegliendo il simbolo più appropriato.**

During your oral presentation, how well did you use your:

1 voice? 🙂 😐 🙁
2 body? 🙂 😐 🙁
3 face? 🙂 😐 🙁

Oracy Oral presentation D

Prepare

1 18 **Leggi e ascolta la presentazione.**

LONDON to PARIS by train

by Emily

Do you know you can travel from England to France by train? You don't have to catch a ferry to cross the sea, you can go under the sea in a tunnel! That's what I did when I went to Paris in August. It was an exciting journey. This is the story of my first trip to France.

We caught the train to London from the station where I live. That was a short journey of about forty minutes. Then we had to get from Waterloo Station to St Pancras International so we caught the underground. It wasn't a direct line and we had to change once. At St Pancras International station we caught the Eurostar train to Paris! This station is a bit like an airport because you have to show your passport and you have to book your seats on the train. Luckily, my seat was by a window so I could see everything. Eurostar is the fastest train service in the UK. The trains are very modern and they don't have to stop at many stations.

The train journey from London to Paris only took two and a half hours! Before the trip, I was a bit scared about going in the tunnel under the sea, but it was fine – it's just very dark. Then suddenly you come out of the tunnel and you're in France! From the train window, France looks different from England! I love visiting new places!

When the train stopped, I was at Gare du Nord station in the centre of Paris! We spent two days sightseeing in the city – it's a beautiful city – and then we caught the Eurostar train back to London. It was a fantastic journey – you must try it!

Area socio-emotiva

Presentation SKILL

Essere preparati a rispondere a domande

Durante la presentazione orale i tuoi insegnanti ti faranno delle domande. Pensa a quali potrebbero essere e preparati a rispondere.

2 Rileggi la presentazione e abbina le due metà delle frasi.

E	Emily went from London	**A**	the train journey.
1 ___	She travelled	**B**	sightseeing.
2 ___	She enjoyed	**C**	by train.
3 ___	In Paris, she went	**D**	wonderful trip.
4 ___	It was a	**E**	to Paris.

3 Rileggi la presentazione e rispondi alle domande.

1. How did Emily travel between stations in London?
2. Is St Pancras International an ordinary station?
3. How long does the journey from London to Paris take?
4. Which station do Eurostar trains arrive at in Paris?

TIPS

Usare i verbi di obbligo

Quando durante una presentazione orale descrivi un viaggio o come fare una determinata cosa, ricordati di usare i verbi di obbligo, come *must* e *have to*.

4 Rileggi il secondo paragrafo della presentazione e trova i verbi di obbligo usati.

1 ____________ 4 ____________
2 ____________ 5 ____________
3 ____________

Research, plan and write

5 Scegli un viaggio che hai fatto e che ti ha colpita/o molto: era lungo, entusiasmante, interessante, difficile?

6 Scrivi il titolo del viaggio al centro della mappa. Poi completala con le tue idee. Trova alcune immagini legate al viaggio.

1. The start of the trip
2. Different types of transport
3. The route
4. The end of the trip

7 Ora sfrutta gli appunti presi nell'es. 6 per scrivere ciò che vuoi esporre nella tua presentazione orale. Usa il testo dell'es. 1 come modello e i box *Presentation skill* e *Tips*. Aggiungi le immagini scelte. Ricordati di includere le tue impressioni e opinioni sul viaggio.

Speaking: Practise and present

8 Prova a leggere la presentazione ad alta voce più volte, poi registrala o fanne un video.

Evaluate

9 Ascolta / Guarda la registrazione della presentazione orale e rispondi alle domande.

1 What did you do well?
2 What do you need to improve?
3 How well was the *Presentation skill* used? Tick (✓) the symbol.

10 Leggi il box 4 Area socio-emotiva a pagina 39 e rispondi alle domande scegliendo la risposta più appropriata.

1 How did you feel during your oral presentation?
2 Was your audience interested?
3 Were you ready to answer questions?

Acknowledgments

The authors and publishers acknowledge the following sources of copyright material and are grateful for the permissions granted. While every effort has been made, it has not always been possible to identify the sources of all the material used, or to trace all copyright holders. If any omissions are brought to our notice, we will be happy to include the appropriate acknowledgements on reprinting and in the next update to the digital edition, as applicable.

Key: U = Unit, O = Oracy

Text references

For the Oracy introduction: Mercer, N. & Dawes, L. (2018) *The development of Oracy skills in school-aged learners.* Part of the Cambridge Papers in ELT series. [pdf] Cambridge: Cambridge University Press

Photography

All the photos are sourced from Getty Images.

UA (1–2): pepmiba/iStock/Getty Images Plus; yalcinsonat1/iStock/Getty Images Plus; MediaProduction/iStock/Getty Images Plus; karandaev/iStock/Getty Images Plus; scanrail/iStock/Getty Images Plus; kedsanee/E+; Kuzmik_A/iStock/Getty Images Plus; Evgeny Karandaev/500px; AnthiaCumming/iStock/Getty Images Plus; paci77/E+; dcdr/E+; Alina555/E+; Victor Metelskiy/iStock/Getty Images Plus; gbh007/iStock/Getty Images Plus; RomoloTavani/iStock/Getty Images Plus; MoMo Productions/DigitalVision; Daisy-Daisy/iStock/Getty Images Plus; Michael Dunning/The Image Bank; Hordieiev Roman/iStock/Getty Images Plus; Rawf8/iStock/Getty Images Plus; LysenkoAlexander/iStock/Getty Images Plus; yogysic/DigitalVision Vectors; calvindexter/DigitalVision Vectors; Dimitris66/DigitalVision Vectors; Anastasiia_M/iStock/Getty Images Plus; Mariha-kitchen/iStock/Getty Images Plus; Vima/iStock/Getty Images Plus; dulezidar/iStock/Getty Images Plus; mariolizaola/iStock/Getty Images Plus; Shaiith/iStock/Getty Images Plus; hydrangea100/iStock/Getty Images Plus; RedHelga/E+; October22/iStock/Getty Images Plus; metamorworks/iStock/Getty Images Plus; filo/DigitalVision Vectors; RuthBlack/iStock/Getty Images Plus; **UB (3–4):** SrdjanPav/E+; Monkey Business Images; PeopleImages/iStock/Getty Images Plus; SolStock/E+; Khosrork/iStock/Getty Images Plus; Chris Tobin/DigitalVision; Christopher Hopefitch/DigitalVision; monkeybusinessimages/iStock/Getty Images Plus; SDI Productions/E+; Paula Daniëlse/Moment; Tom Werner/DigitalVision; Westend61; Glowimages; James Woodson/Photodisc; kyoshino/E+; GlobalStock/E+; Image Source; shapecharge/E+; **UC (5–6):** Cimmerian/E+; Peter Dazeley/The Image Bank; eZeePics Studio/iStock/Getty Images Plus; kmaassrock/E+; grafvision/iStock/Getty Images Plus; anmbph/iStock/Getty Images Plus; Pavel Bezkorovainyi/iStock/Getty Images Plus; Beatrix Neuhaus/500px; Malorny/Moment; Francesco Riccardo Iacomino/Moment; SrdjanPav/E+; Sergiy Trofimov Photography/Moment; PT Images; mikeuk/E+; fstop123/E+; Travelpix Ltd/Stone; **UD (7–8):** Bet_Noire/iStock/Getty Images Plus; taist/iStock/Getty Images Plus; ppart/iStock/Getty Images Plus; Peerasak Kamngoen/EyeEm; malerapaso/iStock/Getty Images Plus; Lilkin/iStock/Getty Images Plus; s-cphoto/E+; kamski/iStock/Getty Images Plus; mladn61/E+; Patcharapol Buasawad/EyeEm; ValuaVitaly/iStock/Getty Images Plus; Antagain/E+; Rawf8/iStock/Getty Images Plus; DesignSensation/E+; LUNAMARINA/iStock/Getty Images Plus; Ingus Kruklitis/iStock/Getty Images Plus; Nadzeya_Dzivakova/iStock/Getty Images Plus; Artur Debat/Moment; Deejpilot/iStock/Getty Images Plus; insta_photos/iStock/Getty Images Plus; DonNichols/E+; s-cphoto/iStock/Getty Images Plus; JazzIRT/E+; saenal78/iStock/Getty Images Plus; Johner Images; Westend61; spooh/E+; loco75/iStock/Getty Images Plus; RedBarnStudio/E+; ucpage/iStock/Getty Images Plus; John Keeble/Moment; Marnie Burkhart/Corbis; grebeshkovmaxim/iStock/Getty Images Plus; MarioGuti/iStock/Getty Images Plus; Nerthuz/iStock/Getty Images Plus; keithsutherland/RooM; LeManna/iStock/Getty Images Plus; **OIntro:** Sirikorn Thamniyom/EyeEm; izusek/E+; Inside Creative House/iStock/Getty Images Plus; **OA (1–2):** Westend61; LauriPatterson/E+; **OB (3–4):**Nastasic/E+; **OC (5–6):** R A Kearton/Moment; **OD (7–8):** R A Kearton/Moment.

The publishers would like to extend a special thank you to Elisa Turri for the invaluable feedback she has provided during the development of the Oracy introduction.